CW01514676

LEWES RACECOURSE

A Legacy Lost?

The Falmer Selling Plate 1951
Rum leads into the five-furlong straight but Anglesey wins

Phreestyle Pholios

2013

Copyright © 2013 Cheryl R Lutring

All rights reserved. No part of this publication may be reproduced, stored in a retrieval system, or transmitted, in any form or by any means, electronic, mechanical photocopying, recording or otherwise, without the prior permission of the publishers.

ISBN: 978-0-9569138-4-5

Every effort has been made to identify sources and copyrights, if we have erred please let us know and corrections will be made in future editions.

Rear cover: courtesy of Roger Hoad

Phreestyle Pholios, Alfriston, East Sussex

Printed by Berforts, UK

LEWES
RACECOURSE

A LEGACY LOST?

Cheryl R Lutring

Dedication

To Shaun Spadah and all the horses – champions and
also-rans – whose courage, abilities and efforts have
provided commerce and status for Lewes town,
as well as entertainment, employment, challenges,
companionship, inspiration, excitement and profit
for many people over two hundred amazing years.

Table of Contents

AUTHOR'S NOTE

Little did I imagine the fascinating journey that lay ahead of me when I started the research for this book. I was inspired to undertake it because of the racehorse Shaun Spadah, whose life and gravestone featured in one of my previous publications. Along the way I have encountered numerous kind people, some amazing horses, and fascinating facts.

So this is an attempt to gather together in one easy-access reference work, as many as possible of the fragmented pieces of valuable history connected to racing at Lewes, before time and oversight sideline it into obscurity.

It is not my intention to create a dissertation of racing odds and results, but to highlight the role of racing for the social and economic life of the community.

My only regret is that it is not possible to include every horse, every trainer, every jockey or stable lad, groom or flint picker, course manager, steward or starter, saddler, farrier, loriner, feed and forage supplier, bookie, tipster or punter. For those that are missing because of error, necessity of space, or lack of record, I offer my sincerest apologies.

In addition to museums and libraries I am indebted to many generous individuals: The Lord Rathcreedan, Bob Butchers, Patricia Robinson (nee Rees), Roger Hoad, and so many others who have shared with me their fond – not to say emotional – memories of the sadly missed Lewes Racecourse.

FOREWORD

Cheryl Lutring's history of Lewes Racecourse rekindles memories of part of British racing's lost heritage. At one time Lewes held almost as important a place in the sport as Newmarket, both as a racecourse and as a training centre, and in these pages you will find many fascinating anecdotes about the myriad cast of personalities, both human and equine, with connections to the town.

Great names of the Turf such as Archer, Gosden, Hannon, Jarvis, Masson, Piggott, Rees, Richards and Smyth feature, as well as an equine cast that includes Aggressor, Charlottown, Eclipse, Persian War and the Grand National winner Shaun Spadah among many others. Royalty, aristocracy, artisans and low-life personalities all have their place in these pages, embellished by old photographs which help to give the reader a picture of one of racing's former jewels.

Once a racecourse has disappeared from the public consciousness it is all too easy in the modern world to forget it ever existed, but for those with a nostalgic mind, this book brings to life the town and the racecourse through the changes of two centuries, right up to the present day where it still happily houses several active racing yards whose inmates still gallop on the old turf of the defunct racecourse.

As a teenage boy with a passionate interest in racing, I remember purchasing the first ever copy of *The Sun* newspaper in 1964, but to my eyes the most interesting topic in its pages was the report and results from the last ever race meeting held at

Lewes the previous day. Mercifully only a few other courses have followed Lewes into the annals of racing where they no longer trouble the editors and journalists of the racing press, but anyone with an interest in racing history and, more particularly, the people and horses connected with it, cannot help but derive knowledge and enjoyment from this beautifully researched volume.

Christopher, The Lord Rathcreedan
Chairman, Stewarding Panel, British Racing Authority 2007-2011

March 2013

INTRODUCTION

As the 50th anniversary of the closure of Lewes Racecourse approaches it seems a good time to reflect upon the history of the erstwhile jewel in the crown of East Sussex.

Beautifully tucked behind the increasingly modernised and expanding town, the racecourse at Lewes is still a busy place where the turf of the historic track is in daily training use by several resident trainers. How many abandoned racecourses, one wonders, can claim this distinction ... or indeed can emulate any of the many distinctions accumulated by Lewes over its two and a quarter centuries.

It is usual to start an historical work at the beginning, i.e. from the first recorded notification of the existence of the subject. In this book it seems appropriate to follow that tradition, so we will begin at the starting post with the aim of reaching the finishing line and, as Lewes was a flat-racing course, hopefully there won't be too many obstacles in our way.

It is thought that the name 'Lewes' derives either from the Celtic word meaning 'slopes', or the Saxon word *hlaew* meaning artificial or burial mound – of which there are many in the surrounds including along the access to the Racecourse. However, really the jury is out on the exact meaning as scholars have differing opinions.

On a windy day, the Old Lewes Racecourse braves the gales from the English Channel after their journey across the chilly Atlantic waters. Little wonder it is difficult to keep your feet as you walk the line of the defunct track, bending into the blast, sympathising with the horses that sometimes had to race not only against each other but against the fury of Woden, god of the winds.

Yet again, on a sunny day in August, could there be a finer place? Basking in the solar rays, cooled by a gentle onshore breeze, with views that are second to none, it is easy to imagine the crowds enjoying the racing against the magnificent backdrop. Easy to picture the sunlight and shadows dappling the glossy coats of the speeding athletes, and hear the ancient chalk resounding to the rhythm of their galloping hooves.

A brief detour of the imagination can also conjure the sounds of clashing swords and desperate neighs of horses from another era. For on almost exactly the same spot as the racecourse is the site of the well known Battle of Lewes, a major confrontation of the Second Barons' War, where Simon de Montfort and his Barons challenged King Henry III on 14th May 1264 – 700 years before the closure of the racecourse in 1964.

Though classified as a country course, Lewes was no peripheral backwater, as confirmed by John Rickman's book in 1952, where he details "twenty-five of the leading racecourses" including Lewes among such famous tracks as Ascot, Newmarket and Epsom. Indeed at one point in its history, it was thought Lewes would outrank Epsom.

So why is the racing heritage of Lewes now virtually unknown – even to modern local residents – what are its hidden secrets, which famous hooves have drummed its furlongs, and whose hearts, souls and mortal remains have been left there?

1

FROM THE START ...

Southern England has been endowed with a precious gift from one hundred million years ago. The skeletal remains of billions upon billions of marine creatures, compressed and solidified, rose up out of the sea when the ancient supercontinent, Pangaea, began to split apart into separate land masses.

Gradually they became our distinctive chalk uplands and developed into the landscape features we now know as the chalk Downs – a word derived from the 14th century Old English word *dün*, meaning hill. Initially their sumptuous curves were covered with beech and yew forests which must have been a beautiful sight in themselves. However, with the discovery of the usefulness of flint, lumps of which occurred throughout the chalk, mankind took to the hills and cleared the trees for his settlements and the grazing of his flocks and herds. The combined efforts of the Great Storm of 1987 and the painstaking work of archaeologists, has revealed evidence of the settlements of the Beaker People (around 2000BC) and Early Bronze Age folk (slightly later).

The clearance work of these early settlers was to provide an enhanced environment for flora and fauna of great variety, some of which exists only on the sweeping escarpments. As the chalk is very porous and free draining the turf is kept aerated and dry – a gift for optimal training of horses.

In addition to controlling the scrub, grazing animals fertilised the top soil generously and this combination enabled the development of the short sward, made up of fescues, milkwort, sedges, vetches and clovers, producing a thick springy turf ideal for galloping. Ideal because, strong creatures though they are in many ways, horses carry their weight on relatively slender legs whose joints and ligaments absorb an enormous amount of strain when travelling at speed. A good surface cushions this and reduces concussion in the hoof and joints.

Not only horses appreciate the conditions. The downland of southern England abounds with significant history and a rich assortment of natural life and the area of the Lewes racecourse is no different. For here is a suitable habitat for creatures as remarkable and disparate as skylarks, hares, shrews, hedgehogs, lizards, moles and voles, snails, butterflies, grasshoppers, glow-worms, beetles and bees, not to mention the friend of all soils, the earthworm. The lately reintroduced buzzards also benefit from the open expanse and *a la carte* coney.

~ ~ ~

It is believed that horseracing in Britain was started by the Romans. However, the first recorded race was held by King Henry II in London at a Smithfield fair in 1174. Interestingly, Chester is the oldest racecourse still functioning with its origin around the mid 1500s for which approval had to be gained from the town's Lord Mayor, Henry Gee. That legacy lives on also in our language as we tell our children of the 'gee-gees'.

In the 16th century King Henry VIII added his weight by enhancing his stud programme with the importation of many fine horses, which ultimately led to the development of the English Thoroughbred. Later it was King James I who discovered the charms of the Suffolk area of Newmarket, which was eventually to become the home of the whole horseracing industry. He established a palace in the High Street of the town – now occupied by the Jockey Club – and between his Royal and Masonic commitments, used it as a base for his principal interests of hunting, hawking and racing for which the turf of the surrounding heath was ideal.

The first recorded race there occurred on 18th March 1622, which was a match race between horses owned by Lord Salisbury and the Marquis of Buckingham – the latter won and pocketed £100, a vast sum for the times, the equivalent of over £9,000 today but with more buying power!

Along with the crown and sceptre, King Charles I grasped the reins and horseracing began to take hold with spring and autumn meetings in 1634 and the first Gold Cup contested.

However, Civil War intervened and Charles I lost his head, but upon the restoration of King Charles II racing once more flourished and he instituted the Newmarket Town Plate in 1664, writing the rules himself:

Articles ordered by His Majestie to be observed by all persons that put in horses to ride for the Plate, the new round heat at Newmarket set out on the first day of October, 1664, in the 16th year of our Sovereign Lord King Charles II, which Plate is to be rid for yearly, the second Thursday in October for ever.

This race was first run in 1666 and in 1671 Charles II created history by personally jockeying his own horse. He won, and though the record is not clear, the horse he rode may well have been Blew Capp, who was a successful royal racer at the time. The Newmarket Town Plate is still run annually and is the world's oldest extant horse race.

If governmental track records are anything to go by, perhaps the sport was becoming too popular too quickly with the aristocracy and the general public alike, because in 1740 Parliament introduced an Act designed "to restrain and to prevent the excessive increase in horse racing". It seems this was generally ignored – in the time-honoured fashion of most silly proclamations – and in 1752 the Jockey Club was formed to create and administer rules for British horseracing. It was the sole governing organisation for the sport until 1993 when certain of its duties were signed over to the newly established British Horseracing Board, which is now the British Horseracing Authority (BHA).

Lewes was not tardy in climbing aboard the gravy train and the first racecourse in Sussex was established on ideal terrain a mile north of the town. The earliest written record of racing there can be found in an unpublished diary by Tom Marchent of 1714, though it seems likely that it was being used for racing earlier in the reign of Queen Anne (1665-1714), before the commencement of official record keeping. The four-mile King's Plate was contested at Lewes in 1720 and certainly regular meetings were being held at Lewes by the time King George II came to the throne in 1727.

The August meeting of 1762 held a two mile race where the winner was Lincoln, owned by Mr Wildman, a yet-to-be-named gelding owned by Mr Todd was second and Smiling Sally owned by Mr Blackman came third.

Sixty two years later His Majesty's Plate was dominated by the horses of three Lords: Lord Cavendish's Mina was first, Lord Exeter's Augusta was second and Spermaceti was third for Lord Egremont. Four mile heats were still being run at Lewes in the 1840s.

In 1793 the August meeting listed two races as being held on the 'New Course'. In 1836 'on the new course' was still being added to the day's programme which implies that the old and new stretches were used 'side by side' so to speak for quite a number of years.

Therefore, rather confusingly, The Old Racecourse as it is known today, could be viewed as the New Racecourse. The exact course of the Old Racecourse is perhaps not fully understood in detail, but seems to have been altered to the current situation from a position that was closer to the town. That is to say the run along the southern ridge into the sharpish corner to the west is where it always was, and the homeward run towards the town swung out more along the line of the current six-furlong gallop

which in its upper reaches crosses the access road. O
tarmac road would not have been there in those day
was quite straightforward. Very early illustrations seei
that the finishing line was well to the east (and sl
north) of the then Spittle Mill.

~ ~ ~

According to the records of 1873 the area which
Lewes course formed part of the 15,000 acres of Sussex land
owned by the Earl of Abergavenny (created Earl of Lewes in
1876), along with his estates in Kent, Norfolk, Hereford,
Monmouthshire and Wales. Their family residence was at Eridge
Park and remains so today.

The task of administering the business of the Lewes
Racecourse was undertaken by John Frederick Verrall, of the
long-standing Verrall family whose earlier connections with the
statesman, Thomas Pelham-Holles, Duke of Newcastle, had a
strong influence over Lewes affairs. Amongst other things, the
Verralls were prominent auctioneers of everything from
household goods to property, but John Frederick preferred the
world of racing. He not only managed Lewes but also Croydon
Racecourse and was well known as a racing journalist. In 1877 he
was succeeded by his brother George, who was a partner in Pratt
& Co (see Appendix III). George also managed Gatwick and
Lingfield racecourses, but soon moved to Britain's racing centre,
Newmarket, where he became influential as a racing official.

In the 1930s the privately owned course became incorporated as the Lewes Racecourse Company Limited, still administered by Pratt & Co. This was a time when other private courses were owned by aristocracy such as the Crown for Ascot, the Duke of Richmond for Goodwood, and official entities such as the Jockey Club for Newmarket. Lewes was one of the few courses to have its own members' Club which was known, suitably, as the Southdown.

The lease from the Marquis of Abergavenny to the Lewes Racecourse Company Limited which ran from September 1930 to September 1951 allowed for the running each year of three race meetings of two consecutive days each, the construction of a Totalliser Building and other necessary facilities and to allow the grazing of sheep except on race days. In addition there was to be continued access for horses, pedestrians, motors and carriages. All this for an annual rent of £460 paid twice yearly. Further race days added to the calendar would incur further rental charges and the lease was totally restricted to horseracing. Concurrently plans were afoot for protecting the area via the South Downs Preservation Bill, and one amendment within that called for stopping motor trials on the existing access road and not allowing such trials when the new approach road from Lewes Prison was constructed. These speed trials for motor cars were popular in the 1930s and started many an aspiring youngster in motor racing.

~ ~ ~

For much of Lewes's long history visiting runners had to walk to the race venues as trains and motorised horses boxes did not yet exist. This was true, of course, for horses going to all racecourses. Usually an organised route would be arranged that would take the horses to specific racecourses for suitable races on one large circuit. For example, in just six weeks in 1769 the mighty Eclipse was walked from his home base in Mickelham, Surrey, to race for the King's Plates at Winchester, Salisbury, Canterbury and Lewes.

Restricted to the speed of his groom, a horse would cover approximately 15-20 miles a day and would be put up overnight in the livery stables at wayside inns. All this must have been an onerous responsibility for the groom as it was a time of highwaymen, general outlaw activity and all manner of hazards.

Upon reaching Lewes the arrivals were stabled around the existing racing establishments who made room for them. This practice was continued right up to the end, as Pratt & Co were landlords of some of the training yards and would require that accommodation be made available for visiting horses. It is quite a thought that horses as significant as Eclipse were once housed in the town and graced the turf of the course with their legendary hooves.

It wasn't until 1836 that the first 'horse box' was invented, as depicted in a rare painting at Goodwood House. A wooden, padded van, it was designed to carry two horses and be drawn by six horses, and was developed to help the horse Elis (who had won the Lewes Stakes in that year as well as many other races at other venues) to travel in relative comfort from his home base of Goodwood to Doncaster thus saving him the additional stress of the 250 mile walk. His companion was his training partner, Drummer. The entourage completed the journey in three days with a stopover at Lichfield. Elis arrived at Doncaster in good form and achieved the aim of winning the St Leger.

Later in the 19th century travelling the horses by train became possible with carriages especially adapted for their needs. They would arrive at the railway station and be walked to the venue or the overnight accommodation. It must have been awesome to see the horses of legendary status being led up Station Street and the High Street on their way to the racecourse; or if arriving early making their way through Lewes streets to the stables that were to be their temporary billet.

Of course the same applied to horses from Lewes who needed to travel to other venues. They would be walked to the Station goods yard, loaded on to the special horsebox carriages, then the engine would be hooked up and they would be hauled off on their journey, which was often a longer-than-the-crow-flies trip as railways tend to work to specific routes and schedules rather than expediency. On one occasion an unexpected change of engines separated the wagon of three horses from the carriage of the attendant lads. The horses ended up at the right station, but the human attendants did not! Ultimately they were reunited but the result was that the horses had to be taken the distance from the station to the racecourse facilities in the dark – not a recommended way to move horses!

The development of road transport for horses led to a new business being spawned in Lewes. Specialised vehicles were expensive and it was more practical for trainers to hire transport when they needed it. In the mid 1940s Ken Oughton, the brother of jockey Alan, ran Lone Star Horse Transport which provided this service from South Street. This later developed into WG Transport, with its depot at a yard beside a lovely mansion with fluted pillars that used to stand where the Tesco supermarket is sited at Phoenix Industrial Estate. The tree that stood by the entrance gates of the mansion is still there. In time WG Transport became part of the now hugely successful Richmond Transport based at Epsom, and the horses can expect luxurious air-conditioned lorries with comfortable air suspension!

Jockeys, trainers and owners too have the benefit in more modern times of being transported via light airplane or helicopter between racing venues. In 1933 one trainer flew from his base in Beckhampton to Chepstow to see one of his horses win the first race, and carried on to Lewes for the last race! In 1937 the champion jockey Steve Donoghue flew from racing in the morning in Paris to land on the Lewes course in time to ride in the afternoon. His aircraft caused a great stir among race-goers – and the horses too no doubt.

~ ~ ~

In the beginning there was no such occupation as racehorse trainer, the animals considered swift enough to race were trained at home by their existing groom whose responsibility it was to look after the horses of his employer, be they work horses, carriage horses, hunters or racers.

Racehorse training did not become a dedicated occupation until the middle of the 1800s, when the younger sons of gentry began to take an interest. This raised the profile of racehorse trainer which soon became an acceptable and somewhat glamorous occupation for their ilk.

Gradually it became apparent that conditions in certain areas were better than others for the process of training horses and consequently dedicated stables began to be opened in those regions.

Lewes benefitted from having good downland conditions for long stretches and a variety of gallops as well as the racecourse itself, so gradually the town and surrounds became centred on the resident in-training horses and the commerce involved with them. At any one time upwards of 300 horses could be in training, stabled mostly around the town with some satellite yards in nearby villages, but all would be served by the same retailers and trades.

Being based at Lewes where important races were held 'on the doorstep' was a bonus too – as at least for some of the races on their agendas the horses could race without the need to travel! Also the Lewes horses had the psychological advantage over visiting horses not only because they were racing on familiar ground, but also because the right-hand route of the course meant they were always heading home towards their stables! Any horseman can attest to a horse's cognisance of the direction of home.

Equally important in the development of racing was the production of the Thoroughbred horse. Though it is true to say that racing beforehand was enjoyed with particularly swift individuals of any breed or ancestry, once the Thoroughbred was established the world of racing became his domain. This cannot be a treatise on equine genetic affairs so suffice to say that the newly imported 'hot blooded' stock from the Middle East (Arabians as we know them today) were put to the existing English mares of suitable talents and over time the 'English Thoroughbred' was established. This fast-galloping breed soon became respected worldwide and has gone on to found the Thoroughbred globally.

Nowadays a horse has to be a Thoroughbred registered with the General Stud Book to be allowed to race under British Racing Authority Rules or Jockey Club Rules and as such has completely taken over the sports of steeplechasing and flat racing around the world. In addition the Thoroughbred has been used to impart quality and refinement to a number of existing heavier breeds thereby creating new useful types and ultimately new breeds.

2

A VIEW OF THE COURSE

High on the escarpment of the South Downs, Lewes Racecourse is roughly the shape of a narrow horseshoe. "The charm of the course is undeniable. The skyscapes, spaciousness and the miles of turf which provide some of the best going in the country give Lewes a freshness ....." so said the notable John Rickman in his book of 1952.

The track runs right-handed and 'orbits' the valley known as Cuckoo Bottom which itself is an offshoot, so to speak, of Horndean Bottom. One of its unique charms was that from the stands it was possible to watch the horses line up at the start on the horizon across the valley, and monitor their progress as they galloped along the crest of the downs highlighted by the big sky.

The two mile course must have demanded superb stamina from the horses as the track rises 100ft in the first half mile. Taking a curve to the right, the going undulates, sometimes quite sharply, to its maximum elevation of another 85ft, before turning homeward on a five furlong downhill run which dropped by 63ft. The last hundred yards to the grandstand presented a slightly uphill finish.

However, with the advent of World War I many things were to change, among them the discontinuation of the two mile races, the last one being the Southdown Welter Handicap at the August 1914 meeting. From then on the longest races were one and a

View from the Bend back to the Grandstands and finish. 'Skyscapes and spaciousness' indeed. Note Firle Beacon on the horizon to the left. This picture was taken in 1900 – a time when the race rails were still there and the scrub was not.

LEWES RACE COURSE

half miles. This eliminated the initial long uphill drag, but the undulations, the bend, the camber and the downhill run-in remained the same.

The starting posts for all races whatever their length were accessed by traversing the track in an anti-clockwise direction. Once 'the off' was sounded by the bugler and the tape had sprung up, the horses leapt into races that, depending on the length, required them to negotiate a mix of undulations, a downhill rather sharp bend, a steeply contrary camber and minimal railing for guidance. Combined, these elements made for an interesting ride – particularly if the wind was blowing from the sea, as was often the case.

In his treatise *The English Turf of 1901*, Charles Richardson records that:

"Lewes is just about as prosperous as any South of England fixture. It has spring, summer, and autumn meetings, and is the headquarters of the Southdown Club, a nursery of gentlemen riders which is exceedingly popular with a certain section of race-goers. At each of the three Lewes fixtures sundry events are confined to gentlemen riders, and a majority of these are run over a distance of ground. At the same time the programmes are strong all round, and at the Summer Meeting, which closes the Sussex Fortnight, three important races are decided, in addition to the gentlemen riders' and plating events. The three are the Astley Stakes for two-year-olds, worth something less than £1,000, the Lewes Handicap of

£1,ooo, over a mile and a half of ground, and the De Warrenne Handicap of five furlongs, which forms a sort of consolation stakes to the Stewards' Cup at Goodwood. More than one beaten Stewards' Cup favourite has made amends by winning the De Warrenne Handicap."

When asked what the course was like from a jockey's point of view, most replied that they liked it, "it was a nice little course" and that they "miss it" though it could be a challenge on a rough wet day. However, in his guide *The Race Courses Atlas of Great Britain & Ireland* F.H. Bayles warns:

"The course is unsuited to some horses as it requires a sharp and active animal to win here ... The ground on the straight varies all the way; very careful riding is necessary down the hill. It would be a very good course provided the dips and angles were levelled down more uniformly."

The same tome from 1903 remarks on the peculiarity of Lewes having two finishing posts, an original device to correct advantage/disadvantage caused by the topography of the course.

"The Five Furlong and Six Furlong races start from the same gate. The latter finishes at the second winning post at the extreme end of the paddock. On the first furlong of the run-in is a fall of 10 feet, equal to 1 in 70 and another 20 feet, equal to 1 in 35, on the first quarter mile, continuing on the fall to the dip. The "Bench mark" above the five furlong post is 463, that at the dip is 400. This declares a fall of 63 feet, equal to 1 in 32 on 660 yards. The last 440 yards are up hill. It is rather an easy, yet awkward descent. The five furlongs measures about 1,160 yards. It will be asked, why have two winning-posts? The one great principle of the Hanover Square firm [the management] is to obviate unfairness where it exists. Now it must be admitted that to start a six furlong race round a turn, as was the rule hitherto, is very much against those drawn on the outside. This is unanswerable, therefore the idea of arranging a second winning-post affords a perfectly straight six furlongs. It may not be approved of from a spectator's point of view, but it largely enhances fairness and the chance of each competitor. The rail side of the run-in is much lower and easier. It is not a course on which to rely too keenly on the form."

Mr Bayles goes on to express the view that, "If such good going were only available elsewhere what splendid race-courses England would possess!"

Others asserted that "The course on Lewes Downs is one of the best in England, the going is always good – in fact, the six furlong course is frequently spoken of as the best in the country. ... Luncheon at Lewes is a particularly important feature of the day's work. One's appetite is certain to be very keen, for a more bracing place is not to be found."

~ ~ ~

By today's standards the facilities at the racecourse for horses and people alike were rather spartan. Having been walked up from stabling in the town, horses had to be saddled in open timber stalls or even in the Parade Ring; there was no cover for them at all, before or after a race, so for the lads and grooms there was much standing about holding horses or walking back and forth to the stable yards in the town.

In 1772, when the revolutionary Thomas Paine lived in Lewes, the first stand was built at the racecourse by public subscription and this offered spectators some respite from the inclemency of unsympathetic weather. In the words of Rev Horsfield in 1824:

> "The Race Course, which is about a mile west of the town, and on an elevated portion of the Downs, is justly regarded as one of the finest in England. A commodious stand, commanding a view of nearly the whole course, was erected by subscription in the year 1772. The races are held at the close of July or the beginning of August, and continue three days. The king's plate of one hundred guineas, is run for on the first day. The Lewes Races formerly possessed sufficient attraction to draw together the lovers of the turf from every part of the south, and the presence of his majesty, then Prince of Wales (who took up his abode in the town in the house of T. Johnston, Esq, during the three race days), collected together the greater part of the nobility of the district."

The original stand was rather ingloriously burned down in the early 1840s, probably as the result of revelry rather than intention, but a new one had replaced it by 1874 which itself was further improved and enlarged in 1893. The public arriving on foot could watch the racing from the side of the track, either paying to be in the 'commodious' stand, or in the free Silver Ring, and many just occupied the rail all the way along virtually to the Bend. On the other hand, ladies and gentlemen had the facilities of the Club Lawn and the grandstands, and those who wished to remain with their carriages had their own dedicated area on the other side of the track from which to enjoy the finish.

View from behind the enclosure for carriages over the course toward the grandstands

The approach to the course is via a single track road which potential spectators were alerted would become congested so it was best to plan to arrive early – sounds like everywhere today!

Above: The 'new' Grandstands in 1900

Below: the 'Grandstands' in 2013 – now houses. Terraces and lawns (where the people are stood in the pic above), and a portion of the track are now absorbed in the curtilage of the residences.

3

RACING

In the 1700s there were eleven races of 100 guineas each given by the Crown. These most prestigious events were consequently called The King's Plate, Royal Plate, Queen's Plate, His/Her Majesty's Plate. The right to run these races was distributed throughout the kingdom between Newmarket, Guildford, Norwich, Nottingham, Black Hambleton, York, Lewes, Winchester and Lincoln and for Lewes were initially held in May, but were moved to August, possibly to make a convenient 'double-do' out of the Racing and the Assizes. The King's Plate at Lewes appears to have first taken place in 1718, but the record is quite clear that in 1720 it was won by a horse called Fox and in 1769 by the mighty Eclipse.

A notice in the London Gazette set out the rules and conditions for Lewes Races in 1772 as follows:

THE King's Plate of One Hundred' Guineas will be run for on Lewes
Downs in Susfex, on Thursday the 13th Day of August, by any
Horse, Mare or Gelding, being no more than Six Years old the
Grafs before, as must be certified under the Hands of the Breeders,
carrying twelve Stone, the best of three Heats, round the Course, To be
shewn and entered at Verrall's-Coffee-House in Lewes, on Wednesday
the 12th Day of August, or they are not to run for the said Plate: And if
any Difference arises relating to their Ages, Entering, or Running, the
fame to be determined by his Grace the Duke of Richmond, or whom he
shall please to appoint, according to such His Majesty's Orders as shall be
produced at the Place of Entering or Running for the said Plate.
On Friday the 14th of August instant, will be run for on the same
Course, a Plate of Fifty Pounds, by any Five Years old, Six Years old, and
Aged Horses, Mares, or Geldings, that never won a King's Plate; Five
Years old to carry Nine Stone, Six Years old Nine Stone Seven Pounds,

and Aged to carry Ten Stone. Every Horse, Mare, or Gelding, running for the said Plate, shall be shewn and entered at Verrall's Coffee-house in Lewes, one Week before Running and each Horse, Mare, or Gelding, to pay Three Guineas Entrance, and Two Shillings and Six-pence to the Clerk of the Course. The Entrance Money to go to the Second-best Horse, Mare or Gelding, not distanced, winning one clear Heat before or after the Plate is determined. Every Horse, Mare, or Gelding, so entering for the said Plate, to produce a Certificate of its Age and Qualifications, on the Day of Entrance and to run according to the King's Plate Articles. The Horse that wins this Plate to pay One Guinea and a half, for the Use of Scales and Drum.

On Saturday the 14th of August Instant will be run for on the same Course, a Plate of Fifty Pounds, the Gift of his Grace the Duke of Richmond, by any Horse, Mare, or Gelding, of any Age, bred in the County of Sussex, viz. Aged Horses to carry Twelve Stones, Six Years old, Eleven Stone Eight Pounds; Five Years old, Ten Stone Ten Pounds; Four Year old, Nine Stone Six Pounds, Mares or Fillies to carry Three Pounds less than Horses of the same Age. The test of Three Heats round the Course. Every Horse, Mare, or Gelding, that is to run for the said Plate, must be shewn and entered at Verrall's Coffee-house in Lewes, on Monday the 10th of August, between Twelve and One o'Clock, and Three Guineas Entrance to be then paid, or Five Guineas any Time before Starting. The Entrance-Money to go to the Second best Horse, not distanced, winning one clear Heat before or after the Plate is determined. Any Horse, Mare, or Gelding having won this Plate in a former Year, is to carry 5lb more than any Horse, Mare, or Gelding of the same Age. For every Horse, Mare, or Gelding, so entered, a Certificate must be produced under the Hand of the Breeder, of the Age of such Horse, Mare, or Gelding, and likewise of its being bred in Sussex. No Horse will be deemed Sussex-bred that was not foaled in the County. Half a Crown to be paid at the Time of Entrance to the Clerk of the Course, for each Horse that is to, start; and when the Plate is determined, One Guinea and a half is to be paid by the Owner of the winning Horse, for the Use of the Scales, &c. The King's Plate Articles to be observed in the Running.

Lord G E O R G E L E N N O X
and
Lord P E L H A M

} Stewards

An Ordinary at the White Hart on Thursday, and at the Star on Friday. A Ball on Thursday Night at Verrall's Coffee-house, and on Friday at The Star. [1]

---

[1] An Ordinary is thought to have been a pre-arranged meal, possibly at a fixed price.

The King's Plates were for six-year-olds carrying 12 stone and 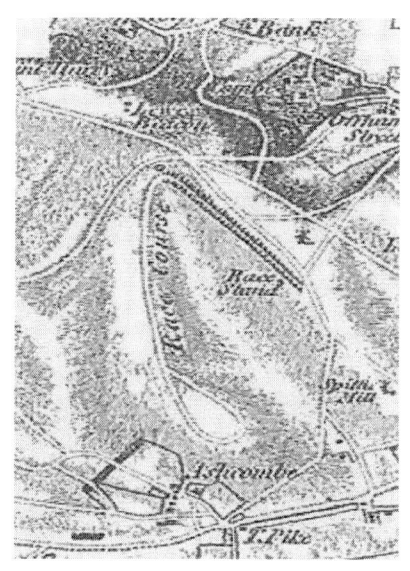being run over four heats, each of four miles. To run a four mile race at Lewes seems to have involved a start on the east side in a counter-clockwise direction, and a swing round the Loop, which is very visible on pre-1800s maps (see left), and return in a clockwise direction to the finishing post. If taken literally the illustration at the top of the race cards in the 1700s also could be indicating a counter-clockwise start.

Lewes staged the eighth running of the race in 1727 when the only contender was the Earl of Halifax's Sampson, a grey stallion.

The next day a purse of 50 guineas was open to any horse that had never won any Royal Plate. They had to carry ten stone. Three heats were contended by Likely a chestnut stallion owned by a Mr Western, Buster a chestnut stallion owned by the Earl of Halifax and Sir William Gage's unnamed chestnut stallion. The race was run over three heats, with Gage's horse being disqualified after heat one, and Likely triumphing over Buster by winning two of the heats.

The 1776 race card for the July meeting lists The King's Plate of One Hundred Guineas on the Thursday, contested by four horses: Enterprize, Kingston, Marshal and Mexico. Next on the card was the Grand Sweepstakes races which attracted runners owned by the Duke of Richmond, Mr O'Kelly of Eclipse fame (see chapter 5), and Lewes's own Sir Ferdinando Poole whose bay colt Criterion came first; Mr O'Kelly's filly by Eclipse won the 100 guineas sweepstake. Next on the card was the Lewes Plate offering Fifty Pounds to be won with one heat, contested by seven runners, with Mr Vernon's grey colt, Thetford, being the victor. Friday was the turn of the Members Plate for Fifty Pounds, with four runners including Sir John Shelley's winning horse Ovid and Sir Charles Bunbury's Glimpse. Saturday was host to the Brightelmston Plate (Brighton Plate) for Fifty Pounds which was run in one heat of six horses; the Duke of Richmond's Plate of Fifty Pounds, again one heat, for which three runners came forward; and Sweepstakes of six runners including Catullus owned by Sir John Shelley.

For that three-day meeting Lord Grosvenor, for example, brought four horses to Lewes, possibly all the way from his training stables in Flintshire. Quite a logistical undertaking for the times!

Another race card from 1786 shows the three-day meeting of July (Thursday 27th through Saturday 29th), starting at twelve o'clock with the County Plate, valued at £50, where the racing was open to 'horses of all denominations' and handicapped by extra weight according to previous wins, genders and ages. The County Plate was contested in four mile heats. Four entries contested the race that day. The Members Plate, again £50, was run on Friday at five o'clock, seemingly the only race that day, which two horses had entered but 'more were expected at the post', implying that entries could be made on the day. The third day started "before dinner" at Twelve o'Clock and featured four races: The Prince's Stakes (Fifty guineas), the Ladies Plate (Sixty guineas), A Plate of Fifty Pounds; then in the afternoon to start at five o'clock the Town Plate (Fifty pounds) for all horses.

~ ~ ~

As with everything in life, the fortunes of a Racecourse tend to go in cycles and Lewes crested the crown of its particular peak in the 1830s and then started to slip down the other side. By 1840 matters had dipped to such a degree that an anonymous poet had the following poem printed in the local newspaper:

> Some thirty years ago or more
> We boasted most transcendent races,
> And the rich course was studded o'er
> With booted beaux and happy faces.
> Then coroneted fours-in-hand
> Were mixed with 'chays' in gay confusion,
> And titled beauties in the stand
> Threw o'er the scene a soft illusion.
>
> Then George Augustus, Prince of Wales,
> Blessed with high health and pristine vigour,
> Gallop'd about our hills and dales
> With many a sporting man of figure;
> And last not least in our esteem,
> A sportsman of the true old school –
> The Lewes Racer's brightest beam
> The good Sir Ferdinando Poole.

Alas! Have changed the picture now.
No carriages! No signs of gladness!
The very cad with low'ring brow
Cried 'Lots of Sport!' in tones of sadness;
The once gay stand was dull as night,
No crowds were formed to push and hustle;
And the lone crow pursued his flight
Heedless of *Rooks* and all their bustle.

Shall good old customs fall and break
Remember life is dull and fleeting.
Gentry of Sussex, rise, awake
Support this ancient County Meeting.
Then will our course resume its spells
The stand again contain its Graces,
And crowds of well dressed beaux and belles
Restore the fame of Lewes Races.

The lamented downbeat period was possibly not helped by the fact that the course fell out of favour with the Prince Regent and therefore he, his entourage and the social elite connected with them, were no longer coming to the racecourse on the Downs. In addition the East Sussex Hunt was disbanded and therefore its Easter Monday fixture was discontinued. This downturn must have had a devastating effect on the economy of the course and the town. In 1847 the Sussex Advertiser's regular column on Lewes Races included the clarion call for improvements. Although the quality of racing was good, and the railway aided transportation, the public were not visiting as they should. Perhaps the clash of the August meeting with the harvest was a factor or perhaps it was that the stand was not so 'grand' anymore and needed refurbishment. After all "we have no title to invite friends if we cannot receive them properly ... let us endeavour to raise a good subscription list and a Grand Stand". At this point it was suggested that maybe an earlier fixture at Whitsuntide would help.

At the end of August 1854 the Sussex Advertiser proclaimed things were now improving and the course would be returned to its 'former glories'. The management had completed the construction of the new grandstand and iron fencing to provide a large saddling enclosure at the front. They had also drafted in the assistance of the illustrious Mr Topham who had sealed his administrative reputation by taking on the floundering Chester Races, dragged them up by their boot laces and set them on the right track, so to speak. Lewes August races were anticipated to provide two days of fine sport and good crowds – as the Brighton & South Coast Railway Company would provide ample transport as well as some sponsorship. The racecourse was deemed to be 'in capital order – better than for years', and the services of Mr Hibburd secured 'whose celebrity as a starter needs no remark'. But, the journalist urges, much depended on the inhabitants of Lewes putting their own shoulders to the wheel and supporting the future of their course.

Maybe it was the improving fortunes of the course that encouraged the Clerk, John Frederick Verrall, to take up the suggestion of an earlier fixture. Seeing that there was indeed a gap in the racing fixtures of the country, he decided to instigate a Sussex Spring Meeting in 1863 to be held on a Tuesday and Wednesday. The report of the meeting was glowing: "His [Verrall's] tact and energy and thoroughly straightforward conduct, which have won for him such deserved popularity, soon brought a large number of sporting friends around him, with promises to enter horses in the races which he might organise. .... The weather throughout the two days was beautifully fine, the sun shining with great brilliancy and a fresh breeze coming over the South Downs rendered the air delightfully cool and temperate. This tempted a large number of metropolitans to the neighbourhood, the Railway Company running special trains for their accommodation. There were no less than 500 persons each day including the leading racing men of the country. In addition the hills were also thronged with spectators. The meeting was highly successful."

It seems John F Verrall was a man of vision and industry, because when taking over his duties as Clerk of the Course, he had encountered difficulty in even staging the normal summer meeting. By the new Spring meeting he had carried out groundworks that included widening the turn, filling in the dip and re-turfing that section, giving the crowd an uninterrupted view of the runners from start to finish. It was said that after this had been done "the ground was equal to any in the kingdom not even barring Newmarket." Praise indeed. In 1873 the course boasted three fixtures a year. Thanks to JFV and his supportive friends, the prosperity of the track had climbed out of the doldrums.

~ ~ ~

The August meeting formed part of the famous 'Sussex Fortnight' which was a sort of festival of racing where horses and punters travelled between Goodwood, Brighton and Lewes. This event featured the most important races on the Lewes card.

The principal race was The Lewes Handicap over 1.5 miles, worth £500 or thereabouts to the winner. First run in 1854, the race has the distinction of becoming the only handicap to fall three times in succession to the same horse. That horse was Rylstone (sometimes spelt Rhylstone) and she won it in 1877, 1878 and 1879. Owned by Lord Hartington (later 8th Duke of Devonshire), she was by Hermit, who was a highly regarded producer of female performers and broodmares. Rylstone also won a handicap at Royal Ascot and the Newmarket October Handicap as a three year old. In 1878, jockeyed by Lewes's own superstar jockey, George Fordham, she took the Kempton Park Cup at the very first Kempton Park meeting. In 1879 she won the Queen's Plate at Doncaster, beating the previous year's Oaks winner by more than six lengths. In honour of this mare a later dwelling at the course buildings was named Rhylstone. Other notable Lewes Handicap winners were Blue Jacket in 1860 ridden by George Fordham and the Australasian horse Merman whose successes also included the Cesarewitch and the Ascot Gold Cup; in 1896 and 1899 it was taken respectively by Paris and Uniform.

First run in 1875 the Astley Stakes, a five-furlong race for two-year olds, was destined to become one of Lewes's prestigious races. In 1880 this race produced one of the most amazing records in the history of racing. A triple dead-heat was achieved by horses ridden by three of the top jockeys of the time: Scobell (Tom Cannon), Wandering Nun (Jimmy Goater) and Mazurka (George Fordham). As if this was insufficient excitement for one day/one race the next placing (officially fourth) was dead-heated by Cumberland (jockey Fred Archer) and Thora. This alone would have catapulted Lewes into the annals of racing history.

The de Warrenne Handicap (five furlongs) – considered one of the top three Lewes races was won in 1884 by a son of See-Saw named Despair.

Race names come and go according to the sponsorship involved. In addition to the Royal Plates, and the races above, other Lewes races have been dubbed: The Town Plate; The County Plate; The Ladies' Plate; The Members' Plate; The Lewes Grand Handicap; Ditchling Stakes; The Priory Stakes (five furlongs); Trial Stakes (1825); The Aristocratic Handicap; The Lewes Stakes, won in 1836 by Elis, who beat the famous Rockingham for whom this was to be the last race of his career, and was won in 1905 by Llangibby when it carried a prize of £2,245; The Queen's Plate (1844 won by Alice Hawthorn); Cuckmere Apprentice Handicap; The Duke of Richmond's Plate (won by Don Dun in 1774); The Castle Plate; Battle Plate; Eastbourne Handicap; Mountfield Court Nursery Handicap; Southdown Welter Plate; Eridge Park Maiden Plate; the Hamsey Welter Plate – a welter race is so named as it is the heaviest weighted race of the meeting[2] – was won in 1885 by a French visiting horse, Monsieur; The Lewes Members' Cup winner in 1930 was Knight of Knockeevan, owned by Albert R McAlpine.

The Eccentric Free Handicap was a mile-and-a half distance race for sprinters which perhaps indicates a certain tongue-in-

---

[2] A weight of 28 pounds (one of 40 pounds is called a *heavy welterweight*) sometimes imposed in addition to weight for age, chiefly in steeplechases and hurdle races

cheek humour at work in Lewes. The inaugural running of this unusual race on 19th August 1872 was won by a bay mare, Lilian, owned by Henry Savile. He had been saving her for that year's Cesarewitch but diverted her instead to Lewes's Eccentric Free Handicap which she cruised by five lengths, in so doing putting not only the prize money of some £150 into Savile's pocket but betting gains of £60,000. In 1874 alone Lilian ran 32 races, winning 21 of them – this being more than most horses could expect to run in their entire careers.

Under the auspices of the Southdown Club, with Pratt & Co as Secretaries, Lewes promoted 'nursery' races for horses ridden by gentlemen. The qualification for these races was that the 'jockey' had to farm a minimum of 40 acres. The Southdown Plate at the June Meeting and the Open Plate and Hamsey Handicap at the Sussex Fortnight meeting, the Ashdown Handicap in the autumn, were part of this policy.

The Eridge Park Two-Year-Old Plate was the very last race to ever be held at Lewes when it carried a purse of £500.

~ ~ ~

Match races had always been popular and Lewes was the venue for many, including some really notable ones, such as that in 1806 between Colonel Melhuish's Sancho and the Duke of Cleveland's Pavilion, ridden by Sam Chifney. These two had contested before at Newmarket when Sancho (the 1804 St Leger winner) had been beaten, so a re-match was arranged at Lewes in the following July, when Melhuish backed his horse at £20,000. The betting caused

Lewes Members Cup won in 1933 by Knight of Knockeevan, owned by Albert R McAlpine

Photographed courtesy of Mr & Mrs David Adam

much excitement as it yo-yo-ed wildly, but rumour spread that Sancho was not on form and Pavilion became the 6-4 favourite. Sancho was partnered by his usual jockey, the very notable Frank Buckle and was holding his own when he broke down in the last mile and was unable to finish, proving rumour right and costing his owner £20,000!

Of such interest was this particular match race that the Prince Regent arrived in a barouche drawn by six matching greys to watch. By noon over 1,000 spectators had also arrived and over the next hour or so the number had reached 3,000. Afterward the royal entourage, including the bereaved Duchess of St Albans, repaired to the Star Inn in Lewes town for refreshment. In the 16th century The Star had been the site of the burning at the stake of seventeen Protestant martyrs; in 1893 it was transformed into Lewes Town Hall.

Originally matches tended to be challenges between two gentlemen who each considered his horse to be the swifter, or perhaps as part of the way of settling a different score between them.In this way racing was occurring much earlier than the record shows, but matches became incorporated into the regular fixtures. As can be seen from the Lewes race card of 1803, the trend appeared to be to hold match races to start the day, and, rather enchantingly after a break racing resumed "After Dinner".

~ ~ ~

Races were started by a tape and a bugle call, not like the starting stalls of today (which were first used in the UK in 1965). Lewes residents recall the starter, dressed in breeches and spats, would ride on a cob[3] to the starting point of any particular race and sound "the off", the lever would be pulled and the starting tape would fly out of the way of the horses as they sprang into action.

from the collection of Bob Cairns

Roger Hoad, who was raised in Lewes – his parents ran The Snowdrop Inn – and has been part of its racing scene all his life, recalls that in his day the cob was called Smokey, and was the hack of trainer Tom Gates. It was Roger's job to prepare the cob in the mornings, and, looking spick and span, take him up to the course, attend to him and the starter during the races, and then bring Smokey home to Leicester Road Stables. He would earn the princely sum of 2s6d for the day's duties – a considerable boost to the weekly wage! But in later years the starter would forsake his trusty cob and do the job from motor vehicles.

---

[3] A small compact sturdy riding horse.

Perhaps a little of the atmosphere was lost when the living spirit of the cob was replaced by inert metal.

In the 1900s the Lewes calendar offered three two-day meetings – July, August and September. In 1962 the very last amateur race was held where the Southdown Welter Plate was won by John Lawrence (later Lord Oaksey) on Dairialtala.

Hopefully this chapter is sufficient to demonstrate that from the outset and over 200 years Lewes Races attracted substantial attendance from the notables in the sport, putting this beautiful course high in the status list of hundreds of racecourses that existed throughout the country.

fco Barbican House

The Lewes Races County Cup was considered 'an excellent test' and 'always an interesting event'. Its trophy was magnificently embossed with scenes of the Battle of Lewes and bearing among its embellishments the coat of arms of Lewes Borough, it is a very fine, ornate silver trophy with a separate lid. In 1868 it was won by King Victor and in 1869 by Queen of Hearts who beat a 'large and brilliant field'. After racing finished the trophy was kept on exhibition at the Anne of Cleves House but, along with other major items, was stolen in 1967. Either desperate or dim, the thief put the trophy up for auction! Inevitably, despite some damage, it was recognised, recovered and restored to Anne of Cleves House where it resides today. This picture is from the days before it was stolen so the Cup is intact.

Racecard from 1803

4

OF PEOPLE PAST

Many colourful characters have spent time working or playing at Lewes racecourse, each notable for their own reasons and in different ways. This chapter takes a look at some of them – in no particular order.

It is generally agreed that Robert Robson (1765-1838) was the very first professional trainer. His early career was in Lewes where he trained for Sir Ferdinand Poole for whom in his first season he produced the Derby winner, Waxy. In an era when trainers usually operated very severe training regimes, Robson refused to race a horse under three years of age, and his innovative approach was more kindly towards the horses in general. As a result even his more sensitive horses would win good races for him. Later he moved to Newmarket and trained several more Derby winners. Among contemporaries he was known as "The Emperor of Trainers".

Sir Ferdinand Poole, part of the vast Pelham family, had the lease of the magnificent house, The Friars, where Waxy was subsequently born. Poole was "of impeachable honour and highly respected", not to say adored by the poor whom he would drive up to the races in his personal and luxurious family carriage, affectionately known by all as 'the tub'. At the Friars he entertained all manner of dignitaries who came to Lewes for the races, including King George III and his entourage. With the advent of the railway in 1846, The Friars was pulled down to make way for the first station. As George Holman in *Some Lewes Men of Note* eloquently put it: "Alas! The good Sir Ferdinando and his ancient residence 'The Friars', have both passed away forever, and the shrieking locomotive now usurps the fields where the generous racer once neighed and curvetted". Later the original station was moved and replaced by the Magistrates Court, which itself has recently been sold off for development.

In July 1791 the super-jockey Sam Chifney rode the Prince of Wales's Baronet to victory in His Majesty's Plate at Lewes. Chifney was not a modest man and proclaimed himself to be able "to ride horses in a better manner in a race to beat others than any other person ever known in my time". Indeed he was not only a skilled jockey hired for life by the Prince of Wales, and winner of most of the important races, but he went on to be a trainer and to develop a new style of bit (the metal part of the bridle that goes in a horse's mouth) which bears his name and is still in use to this day.

Lewes trainer, Thomas Brown was based at what was later to become Astley House, employed at least six lads/jockeys, and produced a remarkable seventeen winners in 1838 alone. Historian T.W. Horsfield writes in 1835 that Lord Egremont had given 'the venerable Mr Brown' one of his best bred stallions to stand at stud in Lewes for the benefit of East Sussex. Indeed Brown had the benefit of several such arrangements with Lord Egremont and stood notable stallions such as the grey St Andrew and Robin Hood.

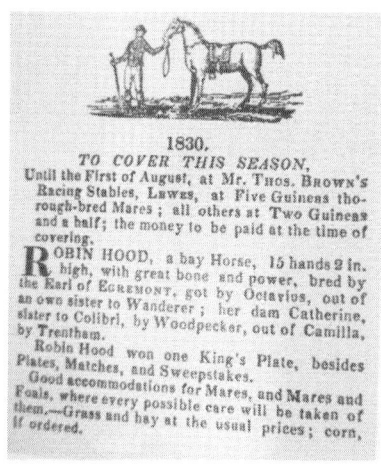

1830,
TO COVER THIS SEASON,
Until the First of August, at Mr. THOS. BROWN'S
Racing Stables, LEWES, at Five Guineas tho-
rough-bred Mares ; all others at Two Guineas
and a half; the money to be paid at the time of
covering,

ROBIN HOOD, a bay Horse, 15 hands 2 in.
high, with great bone and power, bred by
the Earl of EGREMONT, got by Octavius, out of
an own sister to Wanderer ; her dam Catherine,
slater to Colibri, by Woodpecker, out of Camilla,
by Trentham.
Robin Hood won one King's Plate, besides
Plates, Matches, and Sweepstakes.
Good accommodations for Mares, and Mares and
Foals, where every possible care will be taken of
them.—Grass and hay at the usual prices ; corn,
if ordered.

Brown became the subject of a portrait by Archer and a mezzotino engraving by the highly regarded Thomas Goff Lupton.

Brown's grandson, Tom Jnr took on the trainer's mantle and ran the training yard until the property was sold upon the death of his grandfather in 1841, when he moved to the 'superior facility' at Paddock Stables in Paddock Lane, and there stood the famous stallion Alexander the Great. Paddock Stables started life as the stabling for the Haywards Heath stagecoach. Brown was of sufficient national reputation for an 1849 newspaper advertisement for an equine product to cite him as a notable user along with renowned trainers from Ilsley and Lambourn.

The Browns' original yard was sold at auction and purchased by racehorse owner, James S. Douglas of Chilston Park, Kent, who 'much improved it' by demolishing derelict cottages and building a substantial boundary wall. The Sussex Advertiser reported, it would be "an important benefit to the neighbourhood. We understand that an extensive range of stabling is about to be built in addition to the already existing. Mr Douglas has in a short time organized very first-rate training stables, and our town is most fortunate in this property having fallen into such spirited hands. Under the effective management of Mr Drewitt, these stables bid fair to becoming a training establishment of considerable importance." Prophetic words.

The record shows that in 1861 Richard Drewitt's address was shown simply as "105 Spital" which presumably was the site of the later Astley House in Spital Road, Lewes. By that time Drewitt was providing employment for twelve people including grooms, apprentice jockeys and domestics, etc.

The notable sporting patron, Sir John Astley wrote in his memoir that when Drewitt was asked if he was placing a bet on their horse, he would pull down his waistcoat with both hands and reply "Drat it! I won't have anything thank you Colonel; but if he wins, you will have to give the missus a new bonnet." Mrs Drewitt, by all accounts, was a large lady with a good soul and a fine collection of bonnets! Astley also wrote of his decision to send Hesper, his first racehorse, to Dick Drewitt: "I selected Drewitt of Lewes to train him and here I must say a word or two for that honest, good man. He was a particularly careful and good stableman, but knew next to nothing about the handicapping of horses or placing them, nor did he ever bet, and in my humble opinion the above attributes constitute the perfect trainer – at all events to an owner fond of his racehorses, and wishful to keep their merits to himself as well as to ensure getting the best price when he chooses to back them. I don't believe there are any of the Dick Drewitt school of trainers left." Hesper raced until he was 14 years of age winning 20 races and a total of £5574.

One of the most distinguished horses Drewitt trained was Winslow, who at four years old won the Royal Hunt Cup at Ascot in 1873 as well as the Lewes Handicap. He also trained

Lady Mostyn. However, his reputation went beyond horses into the porcine world where he appears to have been something of an expert, often swapping gilts of his favourite Berkshire breed with the gentry.

His yard had a narrow escape in July 1873 when a straw stack caught fire on what was then Spital Farm. Had the wind been from a different direction Drewitt would have been in dire trouble.

Astley House was where James Fordham worked as a stableman, and his son, George, from the age of ten, spent most of his racing career, riding many winners for Drewitt and others. The young Fordham became Champion Jockey from 1855-1863, and riding no less than 165 winners in 1862 alone, his career total to 1881 being 2,382, earning the nick-name "The Demon".

George, "that most famous horseman of all time", was known to be scrupulously honest, quick with humour, kind to new young jockeys, and was completely trusted by his employers. Among other great races in UK and France, he secured the trophy of the Derby in 1879 with Sir Bevys. He married a Lewes girl, Miss Hyde, but after her passing moved back to his home town of Slough where failing health ultimately ended his career. He left a substantial inheritance to his widow (the cousin of his first wife) and their children. On his coffin plaque it states *Tis the Pace That Kills*, which is very appropriate for his life of racing when he often had difficulty making the weight required as his natural weight was only around five and a half stone. When young he and the later-to-be-legendary trainer John Porter would team up and go to pony races on the sands at Littlehampton. John Porter said of

Fordham "he had beautiful hands and horses that stronger men could do nothing with went kindly for him". Sir John Astley wrote of the young Fordham: "an extraordinary judge of pace, was never flurried, and always knew to a nicety where the winning-post was and, above all, was a paragon of honesty".

When it became Drewitt's turn to go to the eternal furlong in the sky, the newspapers reported: "Mr Drewitt who had attained a high reputation of a racehorse trainer, died on Tuesday [3rd November 1874] of the disease prevailing in Lewes." (The nature of the disease is open to speculation!) However, Mrs Drewitt continued the business with a Mr E Caswell training on her behalf. Sadly the Caswells suffered the loss of their five year old son in January 1878.

At the start of his chapter on 'Lewes & Its Country' in his book *Wayfaring Notions* published in 1906, Martin Cobbett wrote: 'I first knew this most ancient borough when Drewitt trained at Astley House, where Escott is now located in a vastly improved establishment'.

Drewitt's main patron, Sir John Dugdale Astley, 3rd Baronet, (1828-1894) and MP for North Lincolnshire, was a prominent horseman usually depicted with a full greying beard and a pipe with a cigar extending from the bowl. Senior Steward for the Jockey Club[4] and owner of many worthy racehorses, he was very keen on both horse racing and boxing and was renowned for winning and losing large amounts at gambling, as well as his

---

[4] Based in Newmarket, The Jockey Club was formed in 1752 and evolved to be the governing body of horse racing in the UK, creating and administering the Rules of Racing.

humour, patronage and turn of phrase. He had quite a quirky character, was known by his nickname 'The Mate', and coined the adage 'like a duck to water' in his book 'Fifty Years of My Life', published in 1895. He often mispronounced his own surname and confusingly referred to himself both in the first person and the third person in the same sentence. On one occasion his watch was lifted from his pocket at Newmarket races, and when recounting the story he said: "Ashley went to the Derby, and I'm blessed if Ashley's ticker wasn't stolen from him. As it had been given to me, and I prized it, I went to the head pick-pocket with whom I was acquainted, and said 'see here, they've taken Ashley's ticker.' The man was very embarrassed and apprehended the thief in his band of brigands and returned the watch with the words "... it was quite a mistake and it was done by a noo beginner"."

Sir John, who died in 1894 aged 66, should also be remembered for his patronage of jockeys, as in 1870 he purchased a property in Newmarket and in 1893 opened it as the Astley Institute for the benefit of the stable lads in the racing town. This is still there and operating with the same ethos though the original building was demolished and a new one built on a slightly different site. He was also a great patron of many sports for all walks of life. In addition to the Astley Stakes at Lewes, he instituted the Astley Belt which was fervently contested in boxing, as well as encouraging and supporting long-distance walking contests.

For a while Lord St Vincent's horses were trained at Lewes by the famously white-hatted Edwin Parr, who earlier had been one of the first trainers to set up at Lambourn. One of his most notable was the 1863 St Leger winner Lord Clifden, a magnificent bay colt whose chances were very nearly nobbled by a youth digging holes in the training gallop. Fortunately the dangerous and dishonourable ploy was discovered and Lord Clifden saved from injury. A special gallop had been made for him away from the eye of the press at Telscombe Village[5], where his workouts would not be so easily observed or reported upon. The St Leger that year was an exceptionally exciting race with Lord Clifden getting off to a very poor start, as was his habit, seeming to stay almost stationary as the others streaked away. He coasted more than a hundred yards behind the field for much of the way, until his jockey, Johnny Osborne, put on the pressure, then systematically the horse turned on his talent and began to reduce the distance and overhaul the other contenders, coming a very convincing first. Lord St Vincent ran down from the stands to greet the victor in the winner's enclosure shouting "I have the best horse in the world". In the later Derby he was ridden by a very confident George Fordham but was beaten by a nose by Macaroni. Indeed both jockeys were convinced that Lord Clifden had won, but the judges thought otherwise. Thereafter that Derby was referred to as 'Lord Clifden's Derby'. Unfortunately, Lord Clifden did not continue to do well and Lord St Vincent became disillusioned and moved from the "Sublime Edwin" to another trainer.

James Prince, who sported bowler hats, trained at Astley House in the 1890s. He was said to be a worthy trainer 'of

---

[5] For further details on Telscombe please see Appendix VII

pleasant disposition and quite a 'good sort' and much esteemed by his large circle of friends and acquaintances ... in consequence of wise management Mr Prince can lay claim to having trained the winners of a very large number of races and certain backers never fail to have a little money on any racing horse prepared by him.' Both he and his brother George had been successful as jockeys but a bad fall at Kempton Park caused James to collapse later. Unconscious, he allegedly laid in the stands for a week. The incident led to him abandoning the saddle for the trainer's togs. But racing was not the only danger; even at home on the gallops it was prudent to be astute. Prince told a journalist in 1891, "we nearly had a smash up at this chain. Five of us were having a trial and had taken down the chain in advance, but on approaching around the curve we saw at the last minute that it had been put up again. We managed to pull to the left and go through the water pit but it was a very near squeak. There were two little boys there and when we asked why they had put up the chain they replied 'we wanted to see you jump it'."

One of Prince's principal patrons was a highly respected, Mr H Heasman, who was known to have an eye for a useful horse. Another was the sporting man and racehorse owner Harding Cox who in 1922 wrote in his book *Chasing & Racing* that his horse Weasel on whom he rode eleven races himself winning eight of them, "was never so well or so carefully trained as he was at Lewes in the able hands of James Prince". By 1911 James had retired, then aged 64, and moved away to Worthing

Mention of Harry Heasman leads us conveniently to an aside about the other aspect of racing – the breeding of racehorses.

Lewes can claim amongst its local breeding establishments the Winterbourne Stud Farm. Here in the 1800s Heasman stood the excellent bay stallion Bartizan whose business diary was limited to twenty approved mares in addition to Winterbourne's own. The foundation mare, Old Druidess, had been a good racehorse herself and was a personal favourite. The horses he bred to race were trained by James Prince, and were popular with the punters as Harry was known as straightforward, honest and good-humoured. Without the breeders neither trainer nor jockey could shine; breeding horses of any sort involves huge investment in money, facilities, time and effort and however knowledgably and carefully planned is very much at the mercy of the random nature of genes.

Contemporary to Prince and a significant Lewes trainer in his own right, was the much-applauded, Dorset-born Harry Escott whose myriad of winners included Cowslip with whom he won at the very first Plumpton Races in 1884. He was also responsible for producing the Grand National winners Lutteur III (1909), ridden by G Parfrement, owned by J Hennessy, and Poethlyn ridden by Ernest Piggott in both 1918 and 1919. He also trained the Grand National third place Pollen and a horse called Troytown who was very successful in major French races. Both were jockeyed by his son Anthony Escott. Newspapers around the world carried the news that a contender for the Grand Steeplechase of Paris was to be trained at Lewes, with headlines typically announcing *'Duettiste in Good Hands: American Champion Jumper to be Trained by H. Escott England's Best'*. Accolade indeed.

Harry had undertaken the bulk of his apprenticeship with James Gatland in Alfriston (trainer of Wild Man From Borneo, 1895 Grand National winner), and later turned to training in his own right at Lewes, operating first from castellated brick stables simply called 'Escotts'. These have long since disappeared, but probably were in North Street where he is listed as having stables at North House. His residence was Hillside, on the Offham Road. By the early 1900s he had moved to the elegant Astley House facility where in 1910 he had 31 horses in training. Curiously, the record shows that at this time one of his jockeys was "in Africa at present". In 1911 he applied to construct additional looseboxes for fifty horses.

Winter exercise on the straw ring at Escotts

Escott had started in business as a trainer in 1885 when he was sent horses by Major Frank B Atkinson, who became a stalwart patron. Atkinson was highly regarded and it was said that no account of the sport of steeplechasing would be complete without including this master of the art. He lived in Brighton and would ride over to Lewes to watch his horses at exercise on the gallops. Harding Cox wrote of Atkinson that he was 'a standing dish at Lewes and successful elsewhere, a very live proposition indeed, and one who could hold his own with the best'.

Escott married twice. With his first wife he had one son, and with his second wife he had two sons and three daughters. His sons Harry Cecil, William and Anthony all became jockeys. Although perhaps somewhat taciturn in character, Escott would participate in community events such as the athletics day at Lewes's oddly named but ancient recreational area, The Dripping Pan. On a wet inclement September day in 1878 he ran enthusiastically in a race of 110 yards with twenty-two entrants. In his heat he drew for first place; but, like fellow contestant John Pelham, did not feature in the run-off! On the occasion of his daughter's wedding, Harry donated a chandelier to St Anne's Church in Western Road in commemoration of her special day – sadly this gift has since disappeared. He seems to have enjoyed an active life until he was approximately eighty-seven and was ultimately interred in Lewes Cemetery. Mr Escott's achievements are such that this book cannot really do him justice.

In 1881 Alfred Sydney trained at Astley House; he is listed as a 'famous Leicestershire racehorse trainer who trained some of the Prince of Wales's horses'. His three sons jockeyed for him and he produced useful winners such as the hurdler Vicar II; Tibocrat, and Stingo by Robert the Devil out of Lady Mostyn.[6] With the help of Annie Huddleston as their cook, he and his wife raised seven children.

---

[6] Robert the Devil was taxidermied and now watches the world go by from his position in Gibson's Saddlery shop window at Newmarket.

Jonathan Riste was a trainer at Heath House (just behind Lewes Prison) in 1896. However, whether from simple bad luck, rashness of character or deficiency in judgement, gambling issues led to his bankruptcy. In 1903 he was refused absolute discharge. The record shows: 'Discharge suspended for four years. Bankrupt to be discharged as from the 11th August, 1907 ... Bankrupt's assets are not of a value equal to 10s. in the pound on the amount of his unsecured liabilities; that he had omitted to keep such books of account as are usual and proper in the business carried on by him, and failed to sufficiently disclose his business transactions and financial position within the three years immediately preceding his bankruptcy; that he had failed to account satisfactorily for any loss of assets or for any deficiency of assets to meet his liabilities; that he had brought on or contributed to his bankruptcy by gambling; and that he had within three months preceding the date of the Receiving Order, when unable to pay his debts as they became due, given an undue preference to one of his creditors.'

Fred Archer (1857-1886) was a very successful jockey who had many of his wins at Lewes, as well as many a drink at the Pelham Arms. Considered by Russell Fox in his book *Scarlett & Silk* of 1896 to have been 'a very delicate man, and, generally speaking, unable to stand even the exertion of a long walk...'. Fox further added, 'but very few have ever shown more power on a horse than he'. Archer certainly proved the point.

Throughout his sixteen year career, he rode 2,748 winners in 8,084 races, but these figures exclude his rides in France and Ireland. In 1885 alone he rode no less than 246 winners, a record that was not broken until Gordon Richards in 1933. Archer was Champion jockey for thirteen consecutive years 1874-1886.

His Classic race wins were:

The Derby	1877	1880	1881	1885	1896	
Oaks		1875	1878	1879	1885	
St Leger	1877	1878	1881	1882	1885	1886
2000 Guineas		1874	1879	1883	1885	
1000 Guineas		1875	1879			

Twice in his career he achieved riding six winners on the same day, once at Lewes when he spent 5th August 1882 in the saddle!

In early November 1886 Archer travelled to East Sussex for racing at Brighton and Lewes, riding Cambusmore in the Autumn Handicap at Brighton on the Tuesday and on Thursday he moved on to Lewes where it was noticed that he seemed not like his usual self, appearing dispirited and unwell, especially after his ride on Lucretius in the Rothschild Plate. His mount for the Castle Selling Plate was Tommy Tittlemouse, a warm favourite. However, they finished very badly and immediately after dismounting Fred said he felt unwell and asked to go home. On his return to Newmarket he took to his bed and eventually his doctor announced that he was suffering from typhoid and that he was restless, seemed disconnected and kept repeating 'I should be dead'. Within a day or so, and certainly before recovering his health, he put a revolver to his mouth and pulled the trigger. The bullet passed through his spinal cord and he died instantly. He was only twenty-nine years of age.

An apprentice jockey from West Wales, Fred Rees came to Lewes originally to work for Ambrose Gorham at Telscombe, who also offered him the chance to be a trainer, but he preferred to ride. With brother Bilbie, Fred moved a few miles northward to the county town of Lewes to ride for George Poole who at the time was based at Astley House.

Fred had a particular soft spot for Shaun Spadah (Horses of Course) with whom he won the Grand National in historic circumstances in 1921 and who he acknowledged as having kick-started his stellar career in horse racing. Called 'the incomparable', Fred was champion jockey five times, clocking up 108 winners in 1924 in an era when there were far fewer fixtures than today and travel to venues was very much slower. All this stardom did not detract from his fondness for Shaun Spadah and he never failed to place a wreath on his grave on Grand National day until his own death in 1955 when his ashes were scattered on Spadah's grave by his daughter Mrs Patricia Robinson. Patricia said to me "I knew Dad would approve as he was very fond of Shaun Spadah. I scattered my husband's ashes there too, and it would be wonderful if I could join them one day".

Fred's glittering career also included winning the first ever race at Fontwell Park in 1924 on 5/4 favourite Gem, and winning the first running of the Cheltenham Gold Cup, also in 1924, on Red Splash. Fred's 100th winner was trained by Gil Bennett in the nearby village of Alfriston for the infamous sporting MP Horatio Bottomley.

In addition Fred won the Grand National, the Scottish National and the French National. These amazing successes made him Champion Jockey for four years and his record for 108 winners was not challenged until after his own death, when in the

1952/3 season Fred Winter took on the laurels achieving 121 winners. Rees was appreciated not only as a great jockey with an empathy for horses but as a smart and amusing man, who, being quite tall, had a constant struggle with his weight. He did his share of war time service, was at Passchendaele as a Royal Flying Corps observer in World War 1, and in World War 2 played his part in the Home Guard when they would ride up to Black Cap and the old racing stables known as Red House, in order to 'guard' Lewes. It is on record that the Lewes Racecourse Platoon was the only mounted one in the entire Home Guard, though they never had need to fire a shot in anger.

Horses were part of the family blood with Fred's brother Bilbie being a successful jockey who won the 1922 Grand National himself just a year after Fred on a horse called Music Hall. He also had the distinction of being the jockey of the legendary Brown Jack when he won the Champion Hurdle at Cheltenham in 1928. Bilbie's son, Dick, was a highly respected equine veterinary surgeon in Lewes in the 1960/70s.

Fred's daughter, Patricia Robinson, was also a keen horsewoman who used to ride her pony Greylight up on to the Downs to watch the racehorses in training. The McAlpine-owned racehorse Knight of Knockeevan, trained by George Poole and winner of the Lewes Members' Cup in 1930, was given to Patricia by way of consolation when her much-loved hunter, Odd Bachelor, was requisitioned by the Scots Greys for war duty – a heartbreaking pointless exercise as the poor creature was sent to Palestine where horses were no longer needed and was probably abandoned there like so many of his hapless fellows.

It seems that George Poole had a somewhat quirky sense of humour coupled with a rather dismissive attitude toward authority. When the racing authorities sent him a letter of gentle reprimand for some misdemeanour, he replied: "Dear Sir, Your letter that was before me is now behind me..." It would be interesting to know what they thought of that response!

After retiring from the saddle, the successful jockey, Tom Thatcher, worked with George Poole. Tom's career had taken him from his home county of Yorkshire to many training yards throughout the country and he had his share of the glory and limelight.

The famous artist, Algernon Fothergill, produced a painting that marked the occasion Thatcher rode Iman to win the first

Tom Thatcher and Iman

race celebrating the completion of the Grandstand at Catterick Bridge in 1906. (detail left/fco J Walker) On this day he was presented with a silver whip by King Edward VII.

While at George Poole's yard Tom was asked to take out a difficult filly to see if he could ascertain why she had caused a near fatal accident to her exercise lad, unseating him, bolting and dragging him for miles with his foot caught in the stirrup. Thatcher took the filly out and found no fault or problem with her. As George Poole's head lad, he was known for being a stickler for correctness, keeping a firm hand on the feed regimes for the horses, often reiterating his favourite mantra: "it's the man with the feed bowl who wins the race". Later he moved to Robert Gore's yard at Findon where he was given a diamond-studded tie pin by the infamously temperamental owner The Hon. Dorothy Paget, who suddenly removed her horses from Gore, but had no quarrel with Tom and told him, "I have nothing against you, Tom, you are brilliant."

What's in a name? Born to a farming and equestrian family of Eastbourne in 1904 John Montague Gosden was dubbed 'Towser' after the family dog ... and the nickname stuck. At 18 years of age Towser visited with George Poole at Heath House, Lewes, and was given the chance to ride out the following morning with a job in the offing if he did well. He did and that very day kicked off his star career in racing. Working at the Heath House stables he learned his craft from what was deemed one of the best jumper-producing teams in the country, led by Poole, of course, and including notables such as Fred Rees, Bill Rees, Billy Spec and Bill Stott. This high calibre experience stood him in good stead for the rest of his life and when he took up the challenge to train on his own (his first owner being the son of Lady Nancy Astor) he was quickly turning out worthy winners. After a short sojourn at Telscombe and then Jevington producing winners for Mr Z Michalinos, his run of success was curtailed by the war. After serving his country during the hostilities, he returned to Lewes and took up the racing mantle again, quickly producing jump winners and developing a string of flat horses, including the highly regarded winner of the King George VI and Queen Elizabeth Stakes, Aggressor. After using a variety of stables in Lewes, he ultimately took on Heath House; it must have been strange for him to be the trainer in the establishment where he had started out! His horses also triumphed in the last two Manchester November Handicaps won respectively by Damredub and Best Song. By 1960 he was third in the Trainers' Table.

One of the Gosden successful apprentices was Jimmy Lindley, who had often partnered Charlottown, and who enjoyed many wins on one of his favourite mounts, Tintinnabulum. Lindley was considered one of the best jockeys of the 1960/1970s but gave up his battle with weight in 1974 and became BBC TV's paddock commentator.

It is one of those unfair twists of fate that, having trained Charlottown through his winning juvenile races including the Solario and Horris Hill Stakes, Towser's health declined to the extent that he was obliged to retire before Charlottown went on to win the Derby in 1966. His retirement led Gordon Smyth from his enviable position as trainer at the Duke and Duchess of Norfolk's private stables in Arundel, to move to the Gosden Heath House facility, where he took over the training of Charlottown in time for the final preparations for his Derby run. Charlottown's win of the great Classic race was a fantastic start for Smyth's Lewes career; but a rather bitter pill perhaps for the ailing Towser.

When Charlottown won the Derby, Smyth treated all eighteen of his stable staff to a celebration dinner at Lewes's White Hart Hotel. Despite a late night and much champagne everyone turned-to promptly the next morning.

Smyth seems to have been something of a character himself. After visiting his training facility at Heath House to assess its suitability, a rather important owner wrote to Smyth saying that he was used to having his horses trained in rather more grandiose facilities. Gordon wrote back politely, pointing out that "if horses are fed well, trained well and looked after well, they will run well and they don't know much about architecture". Succinct and very true – well, he would know having previously been at Arundel Castle stables! Ultimately, Smyth moved to Hong Kong where he trained for many years, but when retirement came he returned to live near Plumpton Racecourse, ending his days there in July 2004 at seventy-seven.

In the late 1930s a certain Tom Masson moved from his farm near Welwyn Garden City to Barn Stables in Lewes. His reputation for bringing out the best in difficult horses led to HM The Queen Mother sending him several of her horses including Edinburgh Festival, Flanders, Gallega and Augustine. Maybe this skill was developed during his years as the trainer of horses for the circus owner Bertram Mills. In the mid 1950s Her Majesty would regularly visit her horses at Masson's Barn Stables (top of de Montford Road) and he would transport her in the back of his old van, where she sat on a tyre, as they laughed and joked their bumpy way to the gallops. Her Majesty Queen Elizabeth II also visited Barn Stables where the horses were paraded for her and she took tea in Masson's modest flat at the yard. Thereafter he treasured with pride the chair she had used.

On average there were sixteen horses in training with Masson at any one time and he was highly regarded by all his apprentices and particularly Bobby Elliott who said: "The guv'nor used to spend hours with them [the difficult horses], just as much time with a horse that couldn't win a seller as he would with a Derby winner. He was very patient and a helluva horseman too."

Another famous owner to visit his horse, Trapani, at Barn Stables was the boxer Tommy Farr. British and Empire Heavyweight champion, the 'Tonypandy Terror', is best known for coming within one point of defeating Joe Louis – a referee mis-judgement that was apologised for in later years!

Masson was always turned out well with shiny boots and spats, plus-fours with long brown socks, tweed jacket with leather elbow patches and a bow tie. His tall, straight posture and neat greying hair finished the look. He always had time to charm the ladies and had a twinkle in his eye!

One of his long-time head lads was Bert Bray; and Masson was the teacher and mentor for many young hopefuls, putting several famous ones on the right path for their successful jockeying careers, including John Hislop, Bobby Elliott, Bob Butchers, Carol Orton, Jimmy Lindley and Dick Francis. The jockey/author Dick Francis rode ponies for Tom when he was very young and Masson is on record as saying "a better pair of hands on a pony I have yet to see".[7] Bob Butchers also acknowledges with respect and affection the influential role of Tom Masson on his riding career. Former champion jockey and breeder of the racehorse star of the 1970s, Brigadier Gerard, John

---

[7] To say a rider has "good hands" is the best compliment they can be paid as sensitive communication with a horse's mouth via the reins is a vital skill.

Hislop said "To his teaching I owed most of any skill or horsemanship I ever acquired."

Sadly, Tom Masson had a car accident in Petworth which left him with fatal chest injuries and he died at Chichester Hospital.

His apprentice in the early 1960s, Bunny Hicks, had his first ride at Lingfield and rose to become Masson's leading jockey until 1968, notably riding Persian War amongst many others, including his first Lewes winner, Nimburg in 1964. Bunny Hicks recalls with some wryness that during his sixteen years as a jockey he rode 50 races at Lewes and only had one win, whereas at Brighton he hardly ever lost!

Tom Masson regarded his apprentice RP 'Bobby' Elliott as "a boy in a million – 99lbs of sheer horse riding genius". When a youngster Bobby had met Alan Oliver, the champion show jumper, who suggested that if he was interested in horses and racing he could do no better than to go to Masson at Lewes. So at age 14, Bobby, along with his brother, did just that.

At age 17, Bobby's very first win of his entire riding career was at Lewes when he romped home by eight lengths on Dante's Inferno in the Ashdown Handicap. Then there was no stopping him – he became champion apprentice jockey in 1959 and 1960 and was retained by HM The Queen as her lightweight jockey. In 1961, on the new saddle given to him by Tom Masson, he was riding Naratious Lad at Hurst Park, when the stirrup iron snapped; without hesitation Bobby kicked off the other stirrup and rode without their support for the entire race ... and won! Bobby rode in five of the six races on that final day for Lewes in September 1964, his mounts were Little George, Monterey,

Dixieland, Enchanted and the winner of very last race, Miss Rhondda, a chestnut mare owned by Mrs L Cohen, trained by Tom Masson and backed at 7/1. After that final race the team all had dinner together and discussed the possibility of taking the winning post away with them as a memento. But in the end they decided perhaps it would be a prank too far. Perhaps they should have been bolder – then we might know the fate of the winning post!

In conversation with Bobby, I asked him what he thought of Lewes Racecourse; he replied: "I liked it, I have fond memories – Towser Gosden, Tom Masson, the Queen Mum's horses – particularly Augustine – I won three for her. She sent her difficult horses to Masson because he was good with them and she used to come down to visit and have tea. Good times."

After his apprenticeship he moved to Lambourn and then spent six years in Hong Kong. Latterly he has taken up training himself in Lancashire. "I'll never retire, I just keep going," he chuckled, proving it by riding out daily even though he turned seventy years of age in 2011.

At Nunnery Stables, trainer G.S. (Jock) Langland had the young Mullens brothers, Alf and Ken, as apprentices. Ken was still at school but preferred his racing duties. Ken's first winning ride was on Truckle at Lingfield and the owner, Sir Malcolm McAlpine, gave him an inscribed watch. Ken became champion apprentice in 1939, 1941 and 1942.

Familiar to all, Gordon Richards rode the first double of his distinguished career at Lewes on 6th June 1921, and fifty years later – to within two days of that date – he won at Lewes with Wild Boy for Lambourn trainer, Bill Payne. In 1937 with British Quota he won the Lewes Handicap in a record time of 2 minutes

Lester Piggott left; Gordon Richards right

31.4/5ths. He also just took the 1950 Newhaven Handicap Stakes (left) pushing Denizen to win by a mere head against the 14 year old Lester Piggott on No Light. Richards became Britain's Flat Racing Champion Jockey for a record 26 times. When he retired from jockeying due to a pelvis injury in 1954 he became a trainer and he and the top jockey Scobie Breasley became an unstoppable partnership. The only jockey (to date) to be knighted, he became Sir Gordon Richards in 1953. He died in 1986.

Most people will know the name of Australian jockey Scobie Breasley but may not appreciate that he rode many races at Lewes and became the course's leading jockey. He also became Champion Jockey in 1957 and again through 1961-1963. The picture overleaf appeared on the front cover of Horse & Hound on 4th June 1960:

Horse & Hound front page photo and caption

"Jockey Scobie Breasley was in great form at Lewes last Monday, having three winners and a second from four mounts. Here he is gaining his third success on Mrs W H D Riley-Smith's Peach Bloom in the Abergavenny Plate, beating Dillingburgh (D Keith) by three lengths, with Vayga (J. Mercer, left) two lengths away, third."

On 6th August 1960 he won no less than five races at Lewes, and it was in July 1961 that Scobie was tricked by a fellow jockey into believing his mount was no threat, but which at the last minute came out of the blue and beat Scobie's horse by a short head. It was taken in good spirit ... jockeys will be jockeys!!

From 1883 George Butchers had been a successful jockey, a career he ran alongside his training business which he commenced in 1893, working out of the Pelham Arms stables – which earlier in 1855 had belonged to Thomas Abrahams, who was also a well known trainer as well as the landlord. Then after a short sojourn at Rottingdean, Butchers returned to his beloved Lewes and trained from Heath House for two years. In 1905 he moved to the stables adjacent to the Black Horse. He won his first race as a trainer with a horse called Beltane, owned by his father. George produced numerous winners for his chief patron Sir Charles Pulley, including Himan (International Hurdle), Marshall Strozzi (Esher Cup), Irish Channel and Grayling IX. He is respectfully remembered for an incident at Plumpton when he was riding Bonnie Scotland for Alfriston trainer, James Gatland. Bonnie Scotland made a jumping error and nearly spun her jockey off over her head. He regained himself only to find that the bridle had slipped from her head and was held in place just by her mouth closed over the bit. In this hapless state, George remained unfazed and set off in pursuit of the pack, taking the lead two furlongs from home, and winning! In 1917 he was appointed private trainer to the beautiful wife of the French millionaire Marcel Varpati, and from their palatial facilities in Norfolk he produced no fewer than sixty-five winners in three seasons. This was all brought to an end in 1920 when Madame Varpati was killed in a motor accident and her grief-stricken widower sold up everything connected to racing. George returned to Lewes and the Black Horse Stables in 1920 to produce more winners for Jack Coltman, including Zarane (who was later given to him) and English Fare who won many races particularly in 1926 and 1927, partnered by the top jockey Harry Wragg. The appreciative Mr Coltman would provide the Butchers family Christmas turkey. Butchers is listed in the Sporting Chronicle Annual as having produced 15 winners who brought home £8,745 in 1911.

George Butchers Jnr, an excellent jockey with a good future, was sadly taken by the First World War, but the second son,

Leslie, was a good jockey too. When George Snr retired, Leslie became the trainer, with the youngest son, Don, acting as chief jockey. Unfortunately Leslie, also, was to fall victim to the long-term damage done to his health by gas in World War I whilst he was serving in Mesopotamia.

After the war the young Don Butchers applied for his own licence and, whilst waiting for it, trained under the licence of Bob Maxwell at Heath House. Maxwell is remembered as a vibrant character, with a big personality, burgeoning sideburns, shiny bald head and always dressed in startling check suits, He had an enormous grin, a penchant for gin-and-tonic and habitually mopped his brow with a gigantic brightly coloured handkerchief.

When his licence came through Don Butchers set up in his own right at Nevill Stables with a mix of jumpers and flat horses. One of his many winners was Be Patient who, jockeyed by the soon-to-be champion jockey Josh Gifford, won at Newmarket.

Don moved to Epsom for a while, taking over from Vincent O'Brien (who was voted the greatest flat and national hunt trainer of the 20th century). While there Don produced the difficult Saffron Tartan to win both the King George VI Chase and the Cheltenham Gold Cup.

Don was respected as a great sportsman who lived up to his principles. He always took a loss with as much grace as a win and is noted for his quiet forbearance when his Carrickbeg suffered a very narrow defeat in the Grand National of 1961.

One of Don's apprentices was the six foot tall Alan Oughton, who married Bilbie Rees's daughter, Diane, and eventually acquired The Vale at Findon where he set himself up as a trainer, producing many winners.

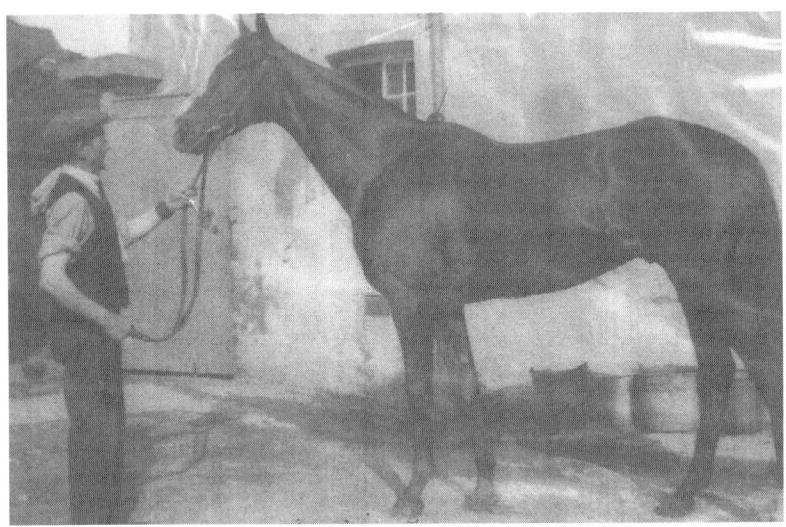

Black Horse Stables' head lad, Joe Keogh, with English Fare who won many races in the 1920s for owner Jack Coltman, jockeyed by the famous Harry Wragg
fco Bob Butchers

In 1924, just a door or two away from Black Horse Stables, a son, Bob, was born into the Butchers family. For much of his youth he worked with Don, but the war was to steer him away from the stables and, after serving in the forces, he returned to civvy street to take up journalism. His racing background proved priceless and he quickly established himself as the original racing correspondent, 'Newsboy', at the Daily Mirror, a position he held with distinction for thirty-nine years. Retired now, he has published his memoir of racing, a comprehensive, insightful, fascinating book called *Silks, Soaks & Certainties*.

Bob Butchers and Greywood exercising on Front Hill Gallop:
left: Alan Oughton on Athelney (fco Bob Butchers)

I had several delightful communications with Bob, who generously shared his memories with me. Among them he recalls that when only nine years old he saw the injured jockey, Alec Cottrill, carried away on a stretcher. It happened in the Hamsey Welter Handicap on 4th August 1933, when the saddle slipped throwing Cottrill under Semiquaver's pounding hooves. He was taken to hospital but died a few days later of his injuries. Seven decades later Bob has not forgotten the tragic sight.

In 1883 another amateur jockey, Captain Hanbury, had been instantly killed at Lewes when inexplicably his horse ran into a post. Reminders indeed, if ever such were needed, that the sport of racing, indeed horse riding in general, is a dangerous one.

Lewes Racecourse was also the venue for a more unusual fatality. Sportsman and author Major Harding Cox, reports in his memoir that in the late 1870s a tremendous thunderstorm broke overhead on a race day with fork lightning cracking and thunder crashing simultaneously. The lightning struck an ill-fated carriage driver, George Avery, ripping through him right down the carriage to the iron tyre which was torn from the rim of the wheel. The driver was killed instantly and it was said that it was possible to see a charred hole in the back of his neck; his garments were tattered and scorched; and the path of the lightning could be followed through the seat cushion to one of the spokes of the wheel. A sobering conclusion to the day's races and, as Cox observed, a reminder of man's audacity in trying to harness the power of nature.

A good friend of Bob Butchers and indeed best man at his wedding, was Matt Feakes. Once the stable jockey for Jock Langland at the Nunnery, and having ridden many horses for Tom Masson, Matt started training on his own account in 1946. Among the forty winners he trained either from his stables at Winterbourne or the Nunnery, was King's Bench, acknowledged as one of the best two year olds in the country, who won the 1951 Emaar Middle Park Stakes at Newmarket, and was second in the 1952 Two Thousand Guineas. Matt was a popular, central figure of Lewes racing life for twenty-four years before he moved to Lambourn in 1954; he died age 89 in 1998.

The Census shows Lester Piggott's grandfather Ernie Piggott as a steeplechase jockey resident at Gateway House, 18 East Street, Lewes. He appears to have been there from at least 1911, and possibly until the Grand National run at Gatwick (the military had snaffled Aintree for the war effort), where he won with the Harry Escott trained horse Poethlyn in 1918. Ernie retired from riding in 1920 and took up training at Letcombe Regis. His grandson, Lester, became multi-times champion jockey, whose riding style changed the look of horseracing thereafter. Lester Piggott first raced at Lewes on 31st August 1948, when he rode Roussel Boy, and his first win there was on 5th June 1950 in the Offham Handicap on Humanity owned by Mr E Thornton Smith.

Yorkshire born, Tom Horney Fitton (right) resided with his wife, Sarah, at 60 Southover High Street, Lewes. His brother, Fred Fitton lived with his wife Ellen, and three children and a cousin, at 41 Southover High Street. Tom is listed as a racehorse trainer with a cousin, Walter, as a stable lad. Tom and Fred trained at Nunnery Stables and in 1915 at Winterbourne Stables. Tom was a trainer of the old school and exercised his horses  over long distances to get them tough and fit. His head jockey at one time was David Dale who later set up on his own at the now lost village of Tide Mills (Bishopstone) in a disused coal yard, working the horses on the shore line and actually swimming them in the sea.

Tim Sullivan was known as a shrewd Irish horseman who liked to play fast and loose with the rulebook for which his jockeys, allegedly, would sometime take the brick-bats if things backfired.

In the 1920s, future trainer Tom Gates acted as George Poole's secretary at Astley House, and would take Grand National winner Shaun Spadah out on the Downs. He also worked for Towser Gosden in the same capacity, and later became a trainer himself at Leicester Road Stables (residing in South Ellis House close by in Prince Edward's Road), enjoying much success and making himself popular by giving after-racing tea-parties for owners and friends. John Slaughter worked for him for eighteen years and has fond memories of those times. "I loved the place and the course; Tom was a special person". This is an opinion shared by many, who mostly describe him as 'a lovely man', 'very laid back', 'a really nice fellow'. Brothers Sammy and Charlie Small worked for him for twenty-five years. Tom trained the horse Proxy, one of the winners in Lewes Racecourse's final season; his very last horse was Welsh Dragon who won a number of races before developing a fatal liver complaint. Tom was also a Special Constable and a very well liked and respected figure among Lewes residents and colleagues. He retired from training in 1975 due to Parkinson's Disease and died some six years later at Hellingly Hospital. The story has it that it was his wish for his ashes to be scattered on Lewes Racecourse and sometime later when the widow Gates steeled herself to undertake this duty, she called around friends and family on a Saturday and said "let's scatter Tom tomorrow". However, sadly that very night she died. A family member stepped in and made sure that Tom's wishes were carried out.

Barred by racing rules and tradition from holding training licences for themselves simply because of being female, lady trainers had to have the licence held by a male – usually either their head lad or their husband. First from Heath House and later in the 1960s from the Nunnery, Auriol Sinclair had been training horses under the licences of Mick Goswell and John Bolton for a long time. Under Bolton's licence she produced among others, the grey Magic Boy who won the Wokingham Handicap in 1958 at Ascot. Thanks to the campaigning efforts of the tireless incognito lady trainer, Florence Nagle, in 1966 the rules were changed and Auriol became the second female in the UK to be granted her own trainer's licence and ultimately became the first lady trainer to produce 100 winners. She had an excellent reputation for being good with three and four year olds, and one of her best known winners, owned by Frank Sanderson, was

Simian who, in 1970, with the assistance of jockey David Moore, brought home the Massey Ferguson Gold Cup from Cheltenham; she also prepared Arctic Actress for the Grand National but had to withdraw the entry as the mare started bursting blood vessels. Auriol also produced the 1974 Cheltenham Supreme Novices Hurdle winner, Avec Moi.

Auriol Sinclair and
Frank Sanderson 1981
fco Val Griffiths

Simian and David Moore on their way to the starting post for the
1970 Cheltenham Gold Cup
photo: fco Val Griffiths

She was born in India at the end of the Raj, and her mother was from the MacFisheries family. Auriol loved cats, particularly the Egyptian and Burmese breeds. Regarded as immaculate and stylish, her London milliner hats were much admired at Royal Ascot.

Among her many claims to fame is the fact that while at Heath House which is adjacent to Lewes Prison, she apprehended an escaped convict with nothing more than her courage and a pitchfork, keeping him cornered until he was re-arrested. Feisty lady.

Believing that the only way to train horses was from horseback, she rode out with two strings every morning. However, over the years she had some bad falls resulting in serious injury such as a broken pelvis and spine; but she always returned as quickly as possible to the saddle. Jo Crowley who worked at her yard for twelve years said: "She was the most amazing person you could ever wish to meet and an excellent trainer." Auriol's secretary of 14 years standing, Valery Griffith said: "I was very privileged to play a part in her very full life. She was a true character in racing." One of the Sinclair stable lads, Nick Davies, went on to become a renowned investigative journalist for *The Guardian*.

Eventually Auriol left Lewes to train privately for Simian's owner Frank Sanderson, chief executive of the Bovis construction group, producing more winners from his Tenterden base. One owner, The Hon Mervyn Greenway had several horses in training with Auriol and said "I've had a number of trainers, but Auriol was the best." She retired in 1985 and died at the age of 81 in December 1999.

Harry Hannon had ridden winners for George Poole before working for Tom Masson, and then in 1948 set up as a trainer in his own right from Nevill Road Stables. Some of his better known horses were Johnny O'Clock and Vera Dunn; and the horse Henri Quatre who won at Kempton Park with the jockey J Hislop aboard. Hannon also trained the 1948 winner of the Brown Jack Handicap at Ascot. Harry's son, Richard and his grandson, also Richard, have carried on the Hannon tradition of horse training with huge success, but now the family is based in Marlborough.

Andy Jarvis had worked in racing since the age of fourteen and had been stable jockey for Towser Gosden. Andy eventually reached retiring age but did not give up horses – he took on the job of driving the dray for Harveys Brewery. His son, Michael, when working for Gordon Smyth, used to take care of Charlottown at Heath House, and had the privilege of leading in the horse when he won the Derby. Michael became a trainer of distinction in his own right, training from Newmarket he produced winners for all the major races right up to 2010. He was a Lewesian of which the town can be mightily proud, as indeed are the legendary trainers John Gosden (son of Towser) and Harry Hannon's son Richard who since 1970 has built up the biggest string in training in the UK – some 270 horses – though not at Lewes!

Chris Hinson who won the Stable Employee of the Year 2007 for his work with Ed Dunlop and the celebrated filly Ouija Board, began his work in horseracing 44 years ago at Auriol Sinclair's Nunnery Stables, signing a seven year apprenticeship which has obviously stood him in very good stead.

Gwyn Hughes Evans trained at Lewes before the war. Described as 'a lovely fellow', he was based at Barn Stables, where he had some horses owned by JV Rank, a prominent racehorse owner and brother of the film magnate, Arthur. Among the most successful horses Gwyn trained was Lacatoi, the only horse to win the Welsh Grand National three times. Unfortunately, Lacatoi's third win was after the tragic death of Evans in a car crash in 1938. Some reports say that Evans's ashes were scattered on the gallops at Lewes even though he had moved earlier to train for Rank in Wiltshire, but this is so far unsubstantiated.

A dynamic and natural jockey, the Irish Henry Robert (Bobby) Beasley, was perhaps known best first for his Cheltenham Gold Cup win in 1959 with Roddy Owen, a horse noted for his quixotic personality, and second for his partnership with the popular grey Nikolaus Silver with whom he won the 1961 Grand National. Upon retirement from jockeying Beasley became a trainer based at the Nunnery in Lewes. In fact he was the last racehorse trainer at that facility. He died in Sussex in 2008.

Born in 1921, the young John Ciechanowski was captivated by racing when Golden Miller won the 1935 Cheltenham Gold Cup. Determined to become a jockey, Ciechanowski spent three seasons as an apprentice with Tom Masson at Lewes, then a further season at the French National Stud before joining the Rothschilds' stud in France. He became champion jockey of France and, in the early 1970s, became an assistant trainer, working in 1973-1976 with Vincent O'Brien. In 1980 he was invited to train for Sheikh Mohammed al Maktoum in Dubai and was responsible for organising the first race meeting to take place in that country. Known as one of the great characters of racing and a true gentleman, he was still riding out at the age of 84, often with a 5:30am start, but sadly died at his home in East Garston in August 2012.

Other trainers who have been based at Lewes include William Downes who trained at the Leicester Road stables he built in 1903 and later at Nevill Road. He was 50 years old at the time of the 1911 Census and his 15 year old son William Harvey Downes was his apprentice. Thomas Smith (55 years old in 1911) who employed Thomas Wyatt as a stableman operated from Winterbourne; Len Hammond in the 1920s; Eric Stedall whose Bois Mill won the Larnach Plate in 1937, and who moved from Heath House to West Ilsley, taking his head lad, Charles McKinnon with him.

The successful French jockey René Emery based himself at Lewes and, after giving up riding, trained at the Nunnery; he was known for his string consisting mostly of greys.

For a long time a major part of the Lewes racing scene, the Moore family returned to UK from the Continent after the Second World War, and first based themselves in Seaford, where Bob was a riding tutor from the Sutton Corner Stables (now gone) and also kept a couple of racehorses. Later he moved to Lewes and took over New Level Stables (aka North Street) and then later moved to Winterbourne. While he was at New Level, Lewes fell victim to one of its famous floods and the stables were awash, with the horses having to be rescued and billeted around other yards, particularly at Auriol Sinclair's, for the duration. The family pony actually swam out of the yard to find firmer footing! Bob watched aghast as all his racing saddles and tack were carried off by the flood waters. His daughter, Barbara Tapp, says of her father, "The life of a racing trainer is a demanding one, but he always made sure that we had Sunday lunch together as a family. Certainly Christmas's were never much as horses that would be racing on Boxing Day had to have full attention and exercise on Christmas Day. When I became engaged father suggested that maybe I would like to consider his and his friend Tom Gates's racing commitments before setting my wedding date!"

Bob was always attended by his little Jack Russell terrier, Trixie, who had a rather unfortunate knack of hiding under the pile of rugs (blankets) when the horses went out for exercise and when she heard the horses returning she would struggle to get

Early Settler, Roger Hoad (up), Bob Moore and Trixie at Winterbourne. Early Settler was generally regarded as 'the best 3 year old' of the era

fco Barbara Tapp

out from under the pile, often would fail but would nevertheless stagger across the yard – a legless pile of moving blankets that would terrify the horses. Bob would always warn of the possibility but many an exercise jockey was caught off guard! There was also a Labrador called Simon who was very affable and allowed anyone into the yard. However, at that point his generosity waivered and he refused to allow anyone – friend or foe – to leave until such time as Bob arrived back and said it was all right. The jockey Alan Oughton remarked ruefully that by keeping him trapped for hours that dog had helped him lose more weight than any other method!

Bob not only trained the highly successful Early Settler, but also the yard favourite, Battle Artist. So popular was this horse with everyone who knew him that when he won a selling race Bob actually purchased him back rather than return home without him and risk upsetting everyone.

Still riding out at age 76, Bob suffered a stroke after morning exercise on 15th April 1973 and died in Victoria Hospital, Lewes.

Another regular sight at the crossing from Western Road over the A277 to the gallops, was Jack Hamilton. His life had always been around the racehorses, working in turn for Tom Gates and Tom Masson, with one of his main functions being 'feed man'. In his semi-retirement, as traffic started to become a risk factor, he would act as 'crossing man' for Towser Gosden's string as they made their way from Nunnery Stables to the gallops, standing in the road flagging down the vehicles with his walking stick. That walking stick had also proved a valuable weapon when a convict escaped from the prison and Jack clobbered him with it thus enabling his re-capture.

The comedy actor of the early 1900s, Tom Walls, seems to have been a busy man. Alongside the stardom of the silver screen, he operated as a jockey and trainer from his base in Epsom, being particularly noted for the Derby winner of 1932, April the Fifth. He is included here because he and his son both rode in the same race at Lewes on 31st August 1932, creating another unusual gem for the record. Tom Snr rode Ballet Dancer to fourth place but apparently his son was not in the frame.

Owners, of course, came from far and wide, some grand, some not so grand, but one or two were actually Lewes people. For example, Solomon Savage, a general dealer and stationer based in Fisher Street, was said to be 'one of the quaintest men who ever owned a racehorse'. At a race in Kent, his horse, Framboise, was in a very close finish where everyone thought he had actually won. But the judge thought otherwise and placed him second despite the protests of the crowd. When the numbers were placed in the frame the band struck up with a vengeance, the crowd surged round and pulled down the winner's number replacing it with that of Framboise. The judge ordered it changed back; the crowd pulled it down again. In the end the judge prevailed but it was indeed a very unpleasant episode. Some years later Solomon Savage ran another of his horses, Adanapaar, at Sandown Park and, against all the odds, won. He is on record as saying that Escott would not lend him a horse to gallop with Adanapaar so he had not really known the horse's ability.

~ ~ ~

The Royal family have long had close associations with Lewes, starting with Queen Anne who, locals assert, enjoyed a ride on the gallops, though like as not this was not on a racehorse.

In 1790, King George III's second son, the Duke of York attended Lewes Races and, with an enviable freedom and good spirit, gave rides in his royal phaeton with himself driving the horses. It is said that thirty people took this rare opportunity and that the Duke was very careful to keep the horses quiet and unmoving while his passengers stepped up into the luxurious carriage and while each group disembarked.

The Prince of Wales (later King Edward VII) – third from the left – watching the races from the private box at the finish line

After a *contra tempt* with the Jockey Club over the placing of a race, the Prince of Wales (later George IV) withdrew from competing his horses at Newmarket, but carried on supporting the 'country races' sending good horses such as Knowsley, to run in heats for the Plates. He particularly liked to send his horses to Brighton and to Lewes, the latter of which was held in 'high repute' and he rarely missed a meeting there. In 1790 his horse Smoker won the 25 guineas sweepstake. Later, when King his presence did much to make Ascot and Goodwood fashionable courses to attend.

In 1835 Princess Victoria attended Lewes Races. Watching the first heat of the first race from their carriage, the royal entourage then moved to the stand that had been specially constructed for them to watch the rest of the heats and take refreshment. Princess Victoria, dressed modestly in pink silk hat and white veil, and wrapped in a Cashmere shawl, returned to the carriage and from there presented a silver bowl to Mr J Ellman of Glynde, the owner of the race winner. In response to the urgings of the 10,000 strong crowd, she stood for a while so they might see her better. Upon resuming her seat the royal carriage moved off through the throng amidst cheers and applause. Quite a day!

HM Queen Elizabeth The Queen Mother would bring her daughters along when she visited her horses at Barn Stables at the top of de Montfort Road. Princess Elizabeth and Princess Margaret, on horses provided by Tom Masson, loved to ride out with the string on the gallops and Downs of Lewes.

In the 1930s there was a familiar cry that used to be heard against the wind at Lewes – "I gotta a horse; I gotta horse" – and a gaudily dressed character would be waving slips of paper in the air and swapping them for cash. The famous tipster, Prince Monolulu, though he claimed to be of Abyssinian royalty, was really no prince at all from Africa or anywhere, but flamboyant he certainly was. His flashy jackets were sumptuously embroidered, his idea of a hat was decidedly individual, and when speaking he often used the 'click' sound used by some African tribes. His real name was Peter Carl Mackay and he would go down into Lewes town into the shops where he had to duck down to get in the doorways, partly because he was a very big man and partly because of his enormous headdress of upright ostrich plumes. He was polite and kind and would buy bags of sweets to take them down to the children at Southover School. Certainly one way to become popular!

Known on both sides of the English Channel and in the USA, he was on good terms with the local punters and racing big-wigs alike, and had the distinction of being the first black man on BBC television when it started broadcasting in 1936. He passed to the great betting booth in the sky in 1965, leaving behind an autobiography appropriately called "I Gotta Horse" and his heavily embroidered apparel which now is exhibited at the Horse Racing Museum at Newmarket.

In 1931 the racing attracted another royal in the form of Prince Aly Khan (son of Aga Khan III) who rode Lights o' London to his first win on the Lewes course.

Even Virginia Woolf took time out from her literary concerns to go to Lewes Races and on 5th August 1932, wrote in her diary of the horses galloping by: "What a noise they made – what a sense of muscle hard and stretched – and beyond the downs this windy sunny day looked remote...."

With all the celebrity and glamour of the high profile people and famous horses, it should not be forgotten that a racecourse and training gallops provide employment for others too. With an average of 300 horses in training at any one time, distributed at stabling throughout the town, there was income generated for many.

There's the course manager who is responsible for everything leading up to, during and after the race day. For much of the time this responsibility was Verrall's or fell to one or other of the partners of the management company, Pratt & Co. In the 1930s the job belonged to a Mr B Maleham whose father was the manager at Alexandra Park racecourse on behalf of Pratt & Co and received a gold watch in appreciation of his fifty years' service. But the last Lewes manager was Jack Cole, who was born in Lewes, but who sadly passed away on 26th June 2011 at age 86, just a few weeks before the start of research for this book.

Then there are the farriers who kept the horses' feet in good order – an important job because as the saying goes "no foot, no horse".

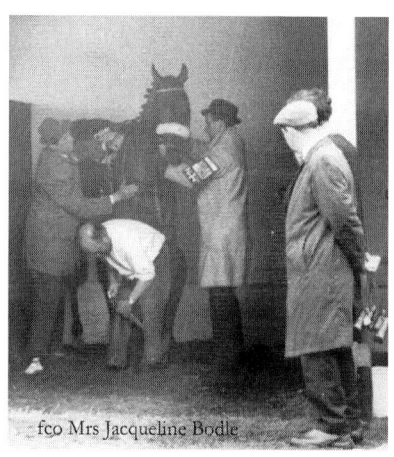

fco Mrs Jacqueline Bodle

George Windless attending to Charlottown at The Derby 1966

George Windless had his forge at the Swan Inn, Southover, and was the routine farrier of Charlottown. He travelled to the 1966 Epsom Derby in the lorry with the horses and the Heath House team, and sure enough his services were required. The horses were parading before the race and the call went out for him to come to Charlottown who had spread a plate.

Re-shoeing was a job done under enormous pressure, as the race was delayed by fifteen minutes while jockeys, trainers, other runners, stewards and starter all waited impatiently, with thousands watching, not to mention having to deal with a horse who could be, to say the least, somewhat energised by the atmosphere and in flighty frame of mind. The nails from Charlottown's offending shoe were kept and remain with the Windless family.

George was a local character who used to travel between yards

George Windless in his Southover Forge
fco Mrs Jacqueline Bodle

on a bicycle, carrying his tools in a bag! He was also a sergeant in the unique mounted Lewes Home Guard and often recalled a two week 'camp' they once had on the racecourse. Trainer Matt Feakes said of him, "What a character! They don't make them like that anymore. He's a craftsman to his fingertips".

Ted Rainbird's forge was at the rear of the Black Horse public house, just on the right up the steps from de Montford Road – very handy for the trainers who occupied the Black Horse Stables!

There were several other farriers based in Lewes town as well, including Ben Stevens in Fisher Street (a forge probably in use for 300 years) and Jack Green; Ringmer Forge had the care of some Lewes horses too and so did Rodmell's amazing Dean dynasty of farriers. Steven Dean remembers his grandfather, Frank, talking about going into Lewes to shoe horses kept in stables in all sorts of places, up alleys, behind pubs, small yards and grand yards "it sounded an amazing place", he said.

Flint pickers, usually local people hired for the duration, walked the course and the gallops removing flints which miraculously popped up from antiquity to sit on top of the grass, again an important job as flints are very sharp and can seriously injure the heels of a galloping horse. There were the gallops men, such as 'Old Mo' Henty in the 1930s, who generally kept the turf in good order. Feed, forage and bedding suppliers – usually local farmers in the past – were of course vital. Veterinary surgeons, stable lads, grooms, secretaries, saddlers and harness makers – Josiah Weller at 31 North Street for example; tailors such as Mr Warner whose shop was called "A Breeches Maker" and John Hother who made breeches in a shop crowned with the royal arms in School Hill in 1870, not to mention the many households who let rooms and board to stable hands and jockeys. On race days there were telegraphists and messengers ... the list is endless and all were essential to the maintenance and operation of a successful racecourse and training establishments, indeed to the commercial viability of Lewes itself.

Even the ubiquitous 'dung heaps' at the training stables were of value and were collected regularly by local farmers who spread them on the land for fertilizer before the advent of less ecological chemical fertilizers, with gardeners and allotment holders seasonally taking smaller amounts for their vegetable plots.

The race days themselves brought hundreds of visitors who spent money on accommodations, food, drink and general revelry over and above the hours of racing. In fact for a very long time

Lewes thrived as a close-knit economic community largely because of the racecourse, particularly in times of austerity in other aspects of life.

The Pelham Arms was a popular watering hole for the Lewes Racing Fraternity when the lads and jockeys would quaff their ales (or lemonade for the really junior lads) in the lower bar with owners and trainers tipping back the spirits in the upper bar. Fred Archer often used to frequent the bar. Pat Caxton, landlady at the Pelham Arms recalled that Charlottown winning the Derby provided a great night of celebration for all when the partying went on until 3am and even the police removed their helmets and joined in. Such was the pride in this racing achievement that the hard-bitten inmates at the Prison were moved to make a large 'Charlottown' banner which was strung across the High Street – a process that stopped the traffic!

~ ~ ~

Of course, there's always ne'er-do-wells and racing was a major 'hunting ground' for the less honest. The racecourses underworld was the territory of gangs running protection rackets, waging razor wars, pick-pocketing and such nefarious activities. London gangs would prowl the courses seeking to gain control over betting and at the June 1936 Lewes meeting thirty of the Hoxton Mob attacked a bookmaker and his clerk with hammers and knuckle-dusters. This resulted in sixteen of them being hauled before the law at Lewes Assizes and sentenced to prison for 43 years.

The on-course feuds between razor villains such as the Hoxton Mob and the Sabini Gang were later recreated by author Graham Greene in his novel, Brighton Rock. The 1948 film of Brighton Rock, starring Richard Attenborough, had sequences shot on location at Lewes Racecourse; and more latterly the course and Roger Hoad's horses and facilities at Windmill Lodge were used for another film, set in the days of highwaymen.

Lewes residents were never slow to enjoy, appreciate and benefit from the activities around horseracing. Race days also created opportunities for those with imagination and initiative.

Houses were opened up to offer accommodation to visitors who would come for the two and three day festivals, hotels and public houses were teeming with incomers and on the course traders of all sorts – from gypsies selling lucky heather to fruit and jellied eels vendors – hawked their wares. Fairground folk would bring along all the fun expected of them and acrobats, musicians, contests of boxing and weight lifting, were to be ogled, laughed at or simply enjoyed. The area around the grandstands would be a mass of betting booths as well as food vendors dispensing jellied eels, peaches and gingerbread. Lewes residents were permitted to set up their own stalls for a very small charge; whilst others had to bid for a place at auction. There was ample opportunity for all to make a gain or two, or simply share in the atmosphere, the excitement, the landscape and thrill of the pounding hooves of the horses.

With a perceptive eye for profit, one lady in Leicester Road would put up a notice at her gate "Ladies Toilet" which was really the privy at the bottom of her garden. Charging simply a copper (a penny in old money) or two, she earned herself some useful extra cash with queues of ladies waiting. This was quite astute because people would have travelled far to attend the races, arriving by train and then having a long walk to the course, where facilities were no better, being temporary screens behind which both genders were invited to: Piddle & Poop A Penny

Race days generated great excitement and children were warned to watch out for all the cars. Crowds of people would be disembarking from the special trains at the railway station and walking through the streets, and Southdown buses would be ferrying people in from the local area and parking up in St Anne's Crescent. For the more energetic spectators there was the opportunity to walk up to the starting posts. To reach the mile start it was possible to follow a short cut down through Cuckoo Bottom and up the other side. This route was popular as along the way was the opportunity to collect blackberries which were turned into jam once back home. Picnics were the order of the day and there was freedom for the children to run around. Boys used to sit at the end of the motor road to the course and watch the vehicles leaving – for nearly two hours – relishing the opportunity to collect licence plate numbers from Southdown, Unique and Banstead coaches as well as private cars. The carnival atmosphere meant the racing wasn't the only thrill of race days!

Other residents recall with affection the strings of horses on Sundays going around the streets of Lewes instead of using the gallops – a quiet day of gentle exercise for man and beast. Most householders collected the droppings the horses left behind as a very cost-effective way of enhancing the fertility of their vegetable plots; children enjoyed the clip-clop sound of hooves and would point smilingly at the passing 'gee-gees'. Everyone knew the jockeys and lads, and took pride in the horses that represented Lewes around the country at major race meetings.

As with any town, residents come and go, families move, the ravages of time take man and memories away. But for some older residents the memories of the racing run deep.

Ivor Wycherley, 90 year old genuine Lewesian, was asked by a journalist what he missed and he replied, "the races, I used to go along and stand by the winning post".

Another resident thought ...

It's very sad to have seen it go ... though with the training still at the racecourse you've got a 'green' type of industry operating and still offering jobs for school leavers. ... For the older type of person born and bred in Lewes racing is a part of them. There's no getting away from that. They remember seeing the horses trotting round the roads and all the people coming on race days, and that's very hard to forget, isn't it? But it's not something you can pass down to children once the horses have gone.

Some pre-closure characters at a Grand National film show at the cinema

Lewes's unique mounted Home Guard (1941) of racehorse trainers, stable lads, apprentice jockeys, and other capable riders. All told some 52 able-bodied and willing 'guardians of the Downs and Lewes', which included Tom Masson, Fred Rees, Ivor Wycherley, George Windless, and known affectionately in the town as the Lewes Cossacks.

5

OF HORSES, OF COURSE

An obvious point, but nevertheless one that must be made: horseracing and all the superstructure around it relies solely on the superb athleticism and generous character of the horse. Seen by some as God's most perfect gift to mankind, the horse never ceases to astound those who know him for the fact that he allows his incredible strength, flighty disposition and superb speed to be harnessed to the bidding of a human – in the case of racing often a very small, slight human indeed!

Many fine and famous horses have set a hoof upon Lewes's downland swells. Their efforts and achievements helped to create the fame and fortune of the town and this chapter is dedicated to them. Unfortunately it is not possible to name them all, but there follows some whose own celebrity perhaps puts perspective into the unique story of Lewes Racecourse.

Eclipse, named for the solar eclipse that occurred in the year of his birth, was set to become arguably the most amazing racehorse of all time. He was a bright chestnut with a narrow blaze, his right hind leg sported a white stocking to the hock. But his temperament was a little uncertain and led many to think he should be gelded, but work put him right, though he did not start until fully mature at age five. He had a peculiar running style, preferring to progress with his nose very low to the ground, a trait that his jockey, John Oakley, managed very well. Eclipse's first race was in 1769 and he won all his nine races that year including the King's Plate at Lewes in July with a new jockey, John Whiting, aboard. Inspired by his phenomenal stamina and turn of speed, owner Colonel Denis O'Kelly remarked "Eclipse first, the rest nowhere". *Nowhere* was the racing phrase used to refer to horses that were a 'distance' (that is more than 240 yards) behind the leader. He won 18 races, mostly by a staggering 10 to 20 furlongs (races were often four miles) and was apparently never fully extended.

He was retired after a very short time mainly because of the lack of competition. Regarded as a super-stallion, Eclipse's descendants make up more than 80% of the world's Thoroughbreds, which includes modern greats such as Kauto Star and Desert Orchid. It was calculated that he raced over 63 miles and walked 1,400 miles to race meetings across England.

Eclipse retired to stud in 1771 at O'Kelly's Stud, near Epsom, Surrey and became the UK's leading sire. In 1788 he was relocated to Cannons Stud, Edgware where, at age 24, he died as a result of colic on February 26, 1789. His skeleton was articulated for display at the Royal Veterinary College in Hertfordshire, and one of his hooves was crafted in gold, prepared as a goblet and given to the King. Hairs from his tail were further woven into the tassel of "The Whip". This was supposedly Charles II's whip, and it became part of the prize of victory in the Eclipse Stakes, along with a framed piece of his hide, and a trophy made from a hoof.

Diomed, the winner of the very first Epsom Derby in 1780, ran his last race at Lewes in 1783, but was not in the frame as he pulled up lame. Owned by Sir Charles Bunbury, the founder of the Classic race The Oaks, he was just six when he retired to stud, but failed to make a big impression and his stud fee fluctuated somewhat. Initially it was five guineas, then rose to ten guineas and ended at two guineas. At age 21 he was to become an emigrant, being sold to the USA to agents looking for English stallions for the American breeding programme. Based at Bowling Green, Virginia, Diomed's fortunes took a turn for the better and, against all predictions, he founded a robust American dynasty which lasted nearly a century and produced horses such as Lexington, star of a mega-era of American racing. When at age 31, Diomed died at Bowling Green in 1808 he was mourned as a national hero and was considered to be a huge loss to American racing and it was reported that "...there was as much mourning over his demise as there was at the death of George Washington."

Foaled at The Friars in 1790, Waxy is one of Lewes's very own super-stars. A grandson of the mighty Eclipse, he was bred and owned by Sir Ferdinand Poole (4th Baronet and Sheriff of Sussex 1789-90) with whom the royal family would dine after the Lewes Races. The Poole horses were trained by Robert Robson who must have been a brave fellow because he bucked the trend by refusing to race two-year-olds, so Waxy did not race until aged three. In 1793 he won the Epsom Derby in June and on 1st August also won a sweepstake at Lewes over 1.5 miles, carrying seven extra pounds due to his Derby win.

A very handsome rich bay, with a white stocking on the off-hind (rear leg on the right side) Waxy was described as having 'good length, especially beautiful quarters, which he transmitted in the highest perfection to his son Whisker'. In 1828 Waxy's exercise rider reflected:

> *"Waxy was one of the finest formed horses, perfect in symmetry, beautiful in colour, admirable in all his paces, and of the finest temper, when in work; but, in the winter, after being weather-bound from frost and snow for some days, on getting out again, it was a case of 'Look out, my boys,' with a vengeance. Oft has he kicked the lappets of my coat over my head."*

Many famous racehorses had companion animals and for Waxy, when at stud in his latter years, this friend was a particular female rabbit who ate oats from his manger and would nestle up to him when he lay down. The doe even made her nest in the middle of Waxy's stall, where she reared many litters which the old horse seemed to regard as his own, often thrusting his nose into the nest to snuffle at the tiny bunnies.

By 1803 Waxy was 13 years old and had lost one eye and soon became totally blind in the other. However, he continued his stud duties and lived to be 28 years old. In the summer of 1804, when Baronet Poole had died, his stock was sold at auction at Lewes, but Robson advised the heir, Sir Henry Poole, that Waxy was too valuable to dispose of, and Waxy remained as part of the Poole estate, although he was moved to Newmarket to the facilities of the Duke of Grafton, where he continued his stud career at an impressive fee of 25 sovereigns. He produced sons who were also Derby winners trained by Robson: Pope in 1809, Whalebone in

1820 and Whisker in 1815. Waxy died on April 10, 1818, and a memorial tablet is fixed on the wall behind the spot where he is buried near All Saints Church in Newmarket. As far as can be ascertained there is no remembrance for him at Lewes.

The issue of naming horses, particularly those of recognised breeds such as Thoroughbreds, can be a complex one. The trend often is to connect the name of the new born foal to the names of his ancestors. This point is made here since Waxy strikes as a rather odd name, but probably came about because Waxy's sire was called Pot-8-Os (potatoes, and originally registered as Potooooooo) and he had an older half brother called Mealy. It will be appreciated that waxy and mealy (floury) are the terms given to types of potato according to their texture; hence the names connect them to their sire, Pot-8-Os.

In King's Plate races, horses carried heavy weights and raced in a series of four mile heats, with the prize going to the first horse to win twice. Sir Harry, at six years old had begun his final season of racing in 1801 and made his first appearance for his new owner Mr Turnor at Lewes in June. Carrying 168 pounds, he ran in three heats, triumphing in the final heat over opponents Warter and Slapbang. He had galloped no less than twelve miles during the afternoon! In August, having raced heavily in the interim, Sir Harry ran his last race in another King's Plate at Lewes, which he lost, and was then retired to stud.

Also in 1801 the well respected black Sorcerer won a four mile sweepstake at Lewes. This was his very last race and he was then retired to the stud of Sir Charles Bunbury, where he produced no less than seven Classics winners, an effort his female offspring continued.

Lewes had the privilege of many Classics winners pounding the turf either before or after their celebrated achievements. For example: the Derby winner of 1805, Cardinal Beaufort (foaled at Lord Egremont's Petworth Park estate) came to Lewes in August and found himself beaten into second place in two races: the 130 guineas Sweepstake and the 60 guineas Ladies Plate.

Election, winner of the 1807 Epsom Derby, ran at Lewes in August 1810 taking the King's Plate on the first day, a 100-guinea sweepstake race on the second day, and on the third day walked over[8] the four mile 60 guineas Ladies' Plate. He came to Lewes again in 1811 but it was not a good year for him and he was retired to stud at the Royal Stud at Hampton Court.

Lapdog, owned by Lord Egremont, won the 1826 Derby and his first scheduled race after that success was at Brighton and then two days later he was at Lewes entered in a Sweepstakes for three-year-olds which he was allowed to walk over as the other entries withdrew because of his presence.

Other good horses were sent to Lewes to benefit from the superb gallops and eminent trainers based there.

---

[8] A walk over was when a horse was uncontested for a race but was required to walk the course anyway to claim the prize. This happened often with horses that were considered unbeatable.

In 1864, Wild Agnes arrived from the north to be trained by John Kent who was then training at Richard Drewitt's yard in Lewes; she was a good racehorse but did not achieve any spectacular or legendary wins, and as a three year old was sold to the Duke of Hamilton.

Drewitt had already trained some worthy winners including Zaidee who won the Norfolk Stakes at Ascot with Fordham aboard in 1856, and Tournament, again with Fordham up, took the 1857 Stewards Cup at Goodwood.

Dick Drewitt also bred Pirate Chief, 1864, at Lewes. Owned by Col. John Astley this horse won three races in eight starts as a juvenile, including a six furlong 100 sovereign plate for two year olds at Newmarket. Unfortunately when a three year old he took a fall in his stable and ricked his back, an injury from which he never really fully recovered but still won again at Newmarket and ran first in the two mile Lewes Grand Handicap. This latter race seemed to confirm his bad luck as the judge had left the box before the horses passed the stand and did not see that some of the runners went off course; the stewards required a re-run and on that time round Pirate Chief lost.

In 1866 another of Astley's string with Drewitt, Actaea, backed at 16-1, won the last great handicap race of the season, The Cambridgeshire at Ascot, against 27 other runners. The newspapers reported 'great rejoicing at his stables when the result became known'. Also at that meeting another of Astley's horses, Ostrager, won the £50 Plate. These horses ran under Astley's pseudonym, Thellusson.

Sainfoin, owned by the illustrious John Porter, had his very first public race at Lewes where he won the Astley Stakes in 1889 carrying 120 pounds, eight pounds more than his rival Garter who he beat by 1.5 lengths. The following year he won the Derby. The Royal Navy ship HMS Sainfoin was named after him in 1943. Recently one of his racing plates (shoe) sold at auction for £500.

Some punters on the 1892 Grand National favoured the not very handsome Cloister who ran at 11:2; but they had not reckoned with the temperamental and self-willed Father O'Flynn (later sent to trainer Harry Escott at Lewes) who was only backed at 20:1. There were some very happy and very unhappy faces in the crowd that day, as Father O'Flynn passed Cloister and romped home 20 lengths ahead of him!

Cloister, described as possibly the 'most amiable horse to ever carry a saddle' did win the Grand National in 1894, but his soundness was in question afterwards and he also was sent to Lewes and Harry Escott, where after a mile workout on the Sussex downs, he collapsed and lay still for some time, with his tongue hanging out. Consequently, he was withdrawn from the next Grand National, and did not run at all that year. The following year, 1896, he was entered for and won both the Welsh Grand National at Cardiff and the Great Shropshire Steeplechase at Ludlow. He was retired having won nineteen of his thirty-five races, and placing second eight times and third three times, being unplaced a mere five times in his career.

Nelly Gray was a good horse at home but tended to be unreliable at racecourses. However, in the Grand National of

1894, she was running at 5-1, the same odds as the eventual winner. Having taken the lead, she jumped wrongly on the second circuit falling back from the front running. When the pack passed her on the second circuit she fell, deposited her trainer/jockey Harry Escott, scrambled up and bolted away. That Grand National was won by Why Not.

According to the racing press, Knight of Rhodes had successes so numerous and "so well remembered that to make allusion to them all is unnecessary". Owned by F B Atkinson and trained by Escott at Lewes, he collected races at Kempton Park, Lingfield Park, and, naturally his home course of Lewes.

Knight of Rhodes held by trainer Harry Escott at his Lewes facility

Escott also trained and rode Cathal, competing in the foggy Grand National of 1895 where they came second to Wild Man from Borneo – a horse trained at Alfriston (seven miles along the Downs from Lewes). With his owner Reggie Ward in the saddle, Cathal also ran in the 1898 National in a snowstorm and again came second. Weather conditions seem to have blighted Cathal's career!

Lutteur III (above) had been bred in France but moved to England and trainer Harry Escott at Lewes from where he was sent out to win the 1909 Grand National. Lutteur's portrait, with his jockey George Parfrement, was painted by the famous horse artist Emil Adam.

During the wartime period, Aintree was requisitioned by the military for the war effort and therefore closed to racing, so the Grand National was moved to Gatwick Racecourse and temporarily renamed The War National.

Again Lewes's Harry Escott features in this renowned race as he trained the 1918 winner Poethlyn who was ridden by Ernie Piggott, the grandfather of the legendary Lester Piggott. Poethlyn won again in 1919 when the race had been restored to its rightful venue at Aintree. It is recorded that he was 'no ordinary chaser but the flower of his [Escott's] stable, where no height, weight or distance could stop his gallop to fame'. Ultimately Poethlyn was returned to his owner, Mrs Peel of Bryn Y Pys Hall, Overton, in Wales where he lived a long retirement. When he died at age 30 he was buried at Bryn Y Pys Hall pet cemetery, alongside the family's champion greyhound, Bryn Truthful. A terrace of eight houses in School Lane is named after Poethlyn.

Another Escott-trained top notch horse was Horizon. Usually carrying the most weight, he would canter to his wins showing his heels to horses with established reputations greater than his own, such as Cloister, the Grand National winner of 1894.

Owned by the celebrated music hall singer, actress and Royal favourite Lily Langtry, the Australian-bred Merman, celebrated winner of the Cesarewitch, Ascot Gold Cup, Goodwood Cup and Jockey Club Cup, won the Lewes Handicap in 1897. The Field magazine reported that Merman, as in the tradition of Australia, ran without plates (shoes) therefore obviously finding himself familiar and comfortable with the hard Lewes ground. Lily Langtry considered him her best horse in her vast string and named her cottage in Beaumont, New Jersey, after him. Another of her horses, Uniform, also won at Lewes in 1899.

Jockeyed by Lewes's very own Fred Rees, Shaun Spadah thrilled the crowds by overcoming difficulties that took other horses off their feet. On a sunny breezy day in March 1921, 200,000 people watched one of the most historic of Grand Nationals. The largest field to start since its inauguration in 1836,

Sir M. McAlpine's "SHAUN SPADAH."

with thirty-five runners, was destined to become notorious for another reason. The heavy going managed to bring down every horse with the very notable exception of Shaun Spadah, a bay ten-year-old, whose betting odds were 100-9 against. Keeping his balance and footing despite two horses falling directly in front of him, he galloped skilfully through the carnage of jockeys and horses strewn in his path and negotiated the loose horses galloping wildly about with reins and stirrups flapping. Yet even he nearly came to grief as he 'pecked' (stumbled) on landing over the water jump, but managed to regain his balance and run on to reach the finishing line first. Only four other horses finished once their jockeys had remounted, and The Bore piloted by Harry Brown crossed the finishing line in second place.

Interestingly, the Jockey Club Rules allowed the remounted horses to finish the race and take their placing without penalty. This rule was not changed until 2009; now jockeys are only allowed to remount in order to return their horses to the stabling.

After his sensational Grand National win Shaun Spadah arrived home by train. He was paraded through the streets of Lewes to cheering crowds lining the route from the station to his home yard at Astley House.

The residents of Lewes were proud of this oddly named gelding and took him to their hearts, for not only had he trained on the gallops behind the town and eaten his oats in a loose box at the stables, but had quietly and steadily triumphed over the carnage that was the 1921 Grand National. After the race Fred Rees thanked the horse for 'cleverly putting his foot out'. A reporter from the newspaper, *Observer*, observed, 'when a less clever animal would unfailingly have come to grief over horses which had come down in front of him, Shaun Spadah changed legs with the agility of a polo pony and galloped serenely on'. In the words of the *Telegraph*'s racing correspondent, 'The freshest horse I've ever seen win a Grand National'.

King George V personally congratulated the jockey, and afterwards when the owner Sir Malcolm McAlpine, (son of 'Concrete Bob' McAlpine) was asked by a Lloyds newspaper reporter about the horse and the race, he replied "I won because I had the best horse, the best jockey and the best trainer."

Shaun Spadah's physical balance and cool thinking approach may have been due in part to his previous sporting experiences. Bred in Ireland, he had made little impression as a flat racer, but instead enjoyed some seasons as a hunt horse. Right minded for the rigours of the chase, he must also have demonstrated a skill for jumping as it was decided that his hooves could be better employed in steeplechasing – a fortuitous change that enabled his skills to be developed successfully.

Having acquired the horse a few months earlier, McAlpine had moved him from Epsom to Lewes in order for George Poole to take over his training in preparation for the Grand National. This was a wise decision as the new training regime and the hilly gallops significantly improved Shaun Spadah's muscle. Poole is credited with 'improving him out of all knowledge', and enjoyed hunting with him as well.

The historic win was commemorated by the jockey receiving an annuity from McAlpine, and a shilling being distributed by George Poole to every elementary school child in the town – a shilling is about 50p in today's money but with a far greater buying power!

Most children immediately spent it on a treat of sweets but the more prudent kept theirs and some still have them today! Then a Lewes resident, Peter Fellows, remembers that his mother was one of those fortunate children... but he is less sure whether she spent the shilling or saved it! So famous did Shaun Spadah become that for a while his name was adopted in Cockney rhyming slang to mean 'motor car'.

Headstone commemorating the burial of Shaun Spadah and ashes of Fred Rees in the Paddock of Lewes Racecourse

British Cartoon Archive, University of Kent, www.cartoons.ac.uk

The meaning of his name is rather obscure, but perhaps Spadah is taken from the Irish word for the special tool used for digging peat; or according to Con O'Leary in his book *Grand National*, Shaun means one who keeps up with the leader in a race, and Spadah means one who the leader cannot shake off! Whatever his name meant, he spent his years of retirement in Lewes and upon his death in 1940 was buried up at the racecourse in what used to be the Paddock. In 1951 he was reunited with Fred Rees whose ashes were scattered on the grave.

The late 1920s and early 1930s were the hey-day of a horse called Andy who was bred and owned by H G Blagrave. A son of Mediator he had a liking for the course at Lewes where he ran no less than fourteen times, winning eight of those races. Millionaire Blagrave was famous at the time for his success rate with breeding, training and racing his own horses. The artist E Craven painted a portrait of the horse in 1930 which may or may not be the work entitled rather unhelpfully "chestnut horse in a stable".

Many notable horses were produced by Tom Masson at Barn Stables, including Cloncarrig, a 1950s Grand National contender who unfortunately fell at the last fence, and the big dark bay Persian War of whom Masson thought very highly. He won at Newbury, jockeyed by Masson's apprentice Bunny Hicks; and triumphed in the 1967 Champion Hurdle as a four year old, an achievement not replicated since 1942; it took a keen purchaser an offer of £9000 to wrest the horse from his owner and Masson – a record price for a hurdler at that time. Also at Barn Stables were Shatter, one of The Queen Mother's horses, who won the 1960 Ascot Stakes ridden by Bobby Elliott; Zarter who became a

Plumpton specialist by winning seven races there in 1951; and not least Pindaric (ridden by Bobby Elliott) and Persian Fantasy (ridden by Stan Smith) were both strong contenders for the 1962 Derby but earned their fame in a different way. As chance would have it the two Lewes horses were involved in one of the biggest pile-ups of Derby history, when seven horses fell – or more correctly were brought down. Pindaric and Persian Fantasy both struggled up and ran on jockey-less, but one horse involved, King Canute, suffered a broken leg and was put down; one jockey was killed and the others were hospitalised except Bobby Elliott who was the only jockey able to be interviewed at the time and he said the others were "in a state of unconsciousness – it was a terrible sight". Such random twists of fortune make all the difference in life and Tom Masson must have cursed his fate that day!

Whyte Warbler is listed here not so much for merit as for her recalcitrance. On a rainy day, ridden by thirteen-year-old Don Butchers back along Lewes's five furlong gallop, the mare took it upon herself to make the decisions. With wet slippery reins, the young jockey was unable to stop her at the end of the gallops and she went on flat out past the prison, down St Anne's Hill, down the High Street, through the narrow bottleneck, to the war memorial where two steep downward hills diverge. Fortunately Butchers managed to point his mare down the slightly less steep Market Street. She kept plunging on until she suddenly found herself in a yard with only some kerbstones between herself and the river, where she stopped dead, ingloriously deposited Don in a heap and stood looking down at him. It's a wonder he ever rode again. Anyone who has experienced a bolting horse will empathise with the chilling vulnerability of the situation.

The powerfully built bay colt, Aggressor, produced by John 'Towser' Gosden, had bettered the Derby winner, Parthia, in the 1959 Hardwicke Stakes at Ascot. Three weeks before the 1960 King George VI & Queen Elizabeth Stakes, he was deemed to be ready to take on the exceptional and favoured filly Petite Etoile[9] who had won the Oaks and was ridden by Lester Piggott. Judgement proved correct and the bay colt beat the grey filly convincingly and raised high hopes for his forthcoming trip to

Aggressor on the rail, ridden by Jimmy Lindley; Petitie Etoile on the right. King George VI & Queen Elizabeth Stakes 1960

Paris for the Arc, but no one told him of the plan and shortly beforehand he reared up in the home yard, fell over backwards and injured his back muscles – an incident that led to an early

[9] In 2012 one of Petite Etoile's racing plates (shoe) sold at auction for £500

retirement for him and disappointment for those around him. Jimmy Lindley tells the tale of the day he was taking Aggressor down the Rhodoendron Walk at Sandown for the Solario Stakes. Suddenly the horse sprang up and over the wall straight onto the bandstand where the band was in full swing; then he swung round, jumped down a four foot drop and slithered across the peat path. Lindley stayed intact in the saddle and thereafter the owner wanted Lindley to ride Aggressor in all his races.

Limited space prevents a countdown of all the winners trained by Towser Gosden, but Charlottown must be included. Bred by Lady Zia Wernher, his training was undertaken at Lewes initially by Towser at Heath House. Having trained the bay colt to a number of wins including the Solario and Horris Hill Stakes, and prepared him for the1966 Derby, Towser was forced to retire due to declining health. Consequently Charlottown was taken over by Gordon Smyth who had started public training at Heath House Stables at the end of 1965. The Derby win gave him a wonderful start at his Lewes base. Upon winning the Derby, jockeyed by the famous Scobie Breasley, he was led in by the soon-to-be-famous Michael Jarvis who was head lad for Gosden and then Smyth. Charlottown became the Racecourse Association's British Horse of the Year for 1966, gaining 176 of the 240 votes; and by the time he retired he was Britain's leading money-earner. So proud were the residents of Charlottestown, Prince Edward Island, of their town's namesake winning the Derby that they presented Lady Werhner with a specially made plaque and an offer of a luxury retirement home for the horse.

One of the horses put in training with Tom Gates had a rather less pleasant reputation. Bistor, from France, had a rather nasty turn of mind coupled with a violent aggressive streak and was not above attacking anyone near him. On one occasion he broke loose, grabbed his intended jockey by a very personal place and, shaking him mercilessly, charged around the paddock. Upon eventually dropping him and promptly knelt on him. Fortunately for humanity, most horses lack this particular attitude.

In 1968 Early Settler was trained for owner the Hon. Guy Butler, by Bob Moore at his Winterbourne base. The lovely grey was by Winston Churchill's stallion Colonist, and was regarded as probably the best four year old in the country, achieving many wins ridden by Lewes jockey, Roger Hoad.

Manhattan Boy, trained up at the Lewes course by John Ffitch-Heyes, then of Grandstand Stables, became a legend at Plumpton. He ran 88 races in his career, 64 of them at Plumpton where he won no less than 14 times setting a record difficult to surpass. Manhattan Boy died at the age of 29 in 2011.

The foregoing is just a sprinkling of the horses, renowned and not so familiar, that have breathed the downland air at Lewes. They and their fellows – often as many as 400 at one time – brought status to the town, cash to the economy and enjoyment not only to race-goers on race-days, but to residents daily as their hoof beats rang through the streets and their power resounded through the chalk of the ancient downland ... and echoes still.

6

THE FINAL FURLONG

Even Lewes's long and illustrious history could not save it from becoming one of the casualties of Levy Board cutbacks. It was announced in 1963 that funding would not go beyond 1966 (ironically the year Charlottown won the Derby!) because of poor facilities and inadequate prize money. At least a dozen good and popular courses including, for example, Manchester Castle Irwell in 1963, Lincoln in 1964, and Rothbury in 1965, also received the closure order.

Re-jiggled fixtures in the mid 1950s meant Lewes ended up with Monday racing which would have done nothing to help take its amazing past into a healthy future, and inevitably it became rather down at heel. As Bunny Hicks confirmed "way behind the times ... for example the great Scobie Breasley, who arrived in a chauffeur-driven limousine, was obliged to hang his Savile Row suit on a rusty nail and change into his silks in the dark and cold; there was no hot water for a clean up after the race, and the toilets were buckets!"

Another problem was the advent of off-course betting shops which meant punters could bet without going near the actual races. Equally, perhaps, television played a part in the decline of attendance at racecourses, though this has undoubtedly recovered now with horseracing being the second biggest spectator sport behind football.

Anyway, big money and fashion had moved off to courses further north and thus, sapped of its life blood, Lewes's situation became dire. No one came forth to offer investment or support, and with lethal accuracy the Levy Board swung its executioner's axe. It is easy in retrospect to suggest that something could have been done to improve matters with a modicum of investment and a mass of commitment, but it was not to be, so the historic track had to accept its fate and the final race day was set for 14th September 1964.

However, the final season of racing proved a good one for local trainers on their own course. Tom Masson produced two winners, including the victor in the very last race; Tom Gates also had two; Towser Gosden two and Bob Moore had one. At the July meeting Lewes lived up to its 'dead-heat' record when

Belinda's Counsel and Orifion in a dead heat.

Orifion and Belinda's Counsel managed to simultaneously breach the finishing line. Orifion, trained by Tom Masson, was backed at 8/1 and Belinda's Counsel, trained by Bob Moore, at 33/1. Must have been an exciting race.

The last season also featured eight-race winner Ron Hutchinson (inducted in the Australian Jockeys' Hall of Fame in 2005), with Bobby Elliot and Scobie Breasley (inaugural inductee into the Australian Jockeys' Hall of Fame) winning four each. Lester Piggott was victor of one race and Masson's apprentice Bunny Hicks another.

The last day itself had a full card and the last race, the Eridge Park Plate for two year olds, was contested by eight runners, jockeyed by famous riders as the results below will show. A crowd of 5,000 turned out to brave a gale force wind to be present on that very last day and to see the illustrious Scobie Breasley ride his last Lewes race, winning the Ditchling Stakes with Beachcomber.

```
2649    ERIDGE PARK PTE (Mdn 2-Y.O.) £345    5f    4.30 (4.31)
918 MISS RHONDDA 9-0
                    RPElliott   (6)  led over 1f out: drvn out—1
20443 Night Signal  8-7¡7       (7)  lw: h: led over 3f: unable
                    BLeyman           qckn fnl f .................2.2
24513 Minyto  8-9¡5 ...JSharman  (8)  no hdwy fnl 2f ...........3.3
2561 Chaplin  9-3  ..RHutchinson (5)  b nr fore: hdwy fnl f: nvr
                                      nrr .....................nk.4
2555 Boodle  9-3 ......ABreasley (1)  wknd over 1f out ......3.5
21633 Kufra  9-3  .........JLindley (3)  nvr nr to chall ..........4.6
2178 FinalBridge  9-0  DWMorris  (4)  outpcd ...................0
      Cariad  9-0  .........BTaylor (2)  w'like: w.r.s: t.n.p .........0
S.P.: 2 Boodle(op5/4), 5/2 Chaplin(tchd9/4), 7/2 NightSignal(op5/1),
7  MISS RHONDDA(op6/1), 9 Kufra(7/1—10/1). 100/8 Minyto, 33
Ors. Tote 21/-: 9/8 15/2 25/4 (112/8). Mrs L Cohen (T Masson,
Lewes) 8 Rn. T/Dble: £20 1s (87 Tckts). T/Trble. £116 11s (8 Tckts)
                                56.5 sec (1.5 under av)   JS
```

fco Don Byrne

The Racecourse Company made no attempt to hide their displeasure at the apparent disregard for their facility and made this plain on the back of the final race card, where they printed:

"It is with the greatest regret that the Management reached the decision that there was no alternative except to discontinue racing after today. Racing has taken place at Lewes for over two centuries

and with crowds of more than 6,000 being attracted to meetings, we believe that Lewes had a useful function to fulfil in British racing, both in providing entertainment for local racing enthusiasts and opportunities for horses not able to compete at top class meetings.

A small racecourse is an essential part of the English racing scene, just as much as it is in other countries such as France where there are nearly 300 courses in addition to the centralised tracks around Paris.

The racecourse is being closed against the wishes of the Management and of many people, who believe that the decision will be regretted in the future. Finally, we would like to thank all our patrons for the support which they have given this racecourse in the past."

The late Pat Mitchell had his own story to tell of the last day of Lewes. He was working for Frank Muggeridge and had the job of leading up Mendrick Court, ridden by a Hungarian jockey who was a Sam Armstrong apprentice at that time. Having released the horse and watched while they cantered to the start he saw the horse deposit the jockey and scoot off down into the scrub and plough of Cuckoo Bottom. The rest of the afternoon was spent with the police, the trainer and the fire brigade looking for the horse. What had been a fine morning turned sure-footedly into a nasty wet, blustery afternoon, when trudging about the Downs was not a pleasure. The horse was not found and Pat suffered mild hypothermia before having to give up at dark. But ultimately the horse was found with his reins tied to a barb-wire fence by someone well meaning but misguided.

Many jobs and livelihoods, not to mention much commerce to the town generally, were lost on that dismal September day in 1964. Along with the horses went cottage industry, sporting status, unique character and an important historic legacy.

The Last Race Card
fco Ian Carpenter

OFFICIAL RACE CARD  **PRICE ONE SHILLING**

LEWES

SEPTEMBER MEETING, 1964
Monday, September 14th

UNDER THE RULES OF RACING

STEWARDS
Lt.-Colonel GILES H. LODER, M.C.
Commander H. S. EGERTON, D.S.C.
Lt.-Colonel C. G. N. TURNER
Sir GORDON MUNRO, K.C.M.G., M.C.

OFFICIALS
Stewards' Secretary—Brigadier S. H. KENT.
Handicapper—Mr. T. W. NAPIER.   *Starter*—Major A. GRAHAM.
Judge—Captain V. D. BURTON.
Clerk of the Scales—Mr. CEDRIC R. MANNING.
Clerk of the Course—Mr. H. C. CLIFTON,
9, St. George Street, Hanover Square, London, W.1.
Veterinary Officer—Lt.Colonel R. H. KNOWLES, M.R.C.V.S.
Medical Officer—Dr. R. CUNNINGHAM-JONES.
Auctioneer—Mr. D. HUBBARD.
Veterinary Surgeon—Mr. J. A. MORRIS, M.R.C.V.S.
Secretaries—
Messrs. PRATT & CO., 9, St. George Street, Hanover Square, London, W.1.

COPYRIGHT
Published by Authority of the Clerk of the Course and printed by
PRATT & Co., Heddon Street, Regent Street, London, W.1.

2.0.—THE CUCKMERE APPRENTICES HANDICAP PLATE

of £500; entrance £2, £2 extra if declared to run by Thursday, September 10th, and £1 in addition unless such declaration be cancelled by Saturday, September 12th; the second to receive £100 and the third £50 out of the plate; for three-yrs-old and upwards; lowest handicap weight not less than 6st 7lb.: weights published Thursday, September 3rd, but the winner after Monday, August 31st, to carry 7lb. of two races, or of one value £400, 12lb extra, to be ridden by apprentices who have not ridden more than three winners (apprentice races excepted); one mile and a quarter (44 entries, viz. 9 at £5, 8 at £4 and 27 at £2).—Closed August 19th, 1964.

Jockey	Age st lb	Trainer	Owner
1	THE WOLF 5 9 8	Mr E. J. Piller	
	b h Hugh Lupus—Fair Amazon	J. Bartholomew	Blue and white check, black cap
2	MISTY RIVER 4 9 5	Mrs R. A. Thrale	
	br br/Herzall/Henry—Shannon Lady	R. Thrale	Pale blue, wide stripe, cuffs and peak of cap
5	WAVE 4 8 13	Mr W. Wadey	
	br g Honeyway—Oure	V. Smyth	Green and white (halved), slvs reversed, quartered cap
6	BUZZ 4 8 12	Mr Vivian Loyd	
	b/Hirnall Honey—Arc Light	S. Ingham	White, green striped sleeves
10	SAUCY LAD 4 8 6	Major Philip Magor	
	b g Democratic—Saucy Maid	T. Masson	Purple, gold star, slvs and hooped cap
11	NIMBURG 4 8 5	Mr R. W. G. Collins	
	b g Fastony II—Moonleys Gates		White, red hooped sleeves, blue and white quartered cap
13	METHANE 5 8 0	Mrs C. Busatilli	
	ch h Mossborough—Coal Board	D. Marks	Red, amber hoop, green cap
14	GREAT LADY 4 7 12	Baroness W. Langer von Langendorff	
	ch f Chanidoy—Russian Row	H. Smyth	Yellow, white epaulets, green cap, yellow star
17	ST. KIERAN 4 6 7	Mr E. J. Cashin	
	ch s Kyalmäite—Fashion Ness	D. Hanley	Violet, yellow sleeves, green cap

NINE DECLARED RUNNERS

TOTALISATOR INFORMATION

Forecast Betting (selecting the first two placed horses): 3 to 6 runners, first two in correct order, 7 to 9 runners, first two in either order (ask for the lowest horse number first).
Place Betting : 8 or more runners, 3 places, 6 or 7 runners, 2 places only.
Daily Treble Event : On the 2nd, 4th and 6th races (5/- unit).
Daily Double : On the 3rd and 5th races (10/- unit).

The Totalisator is operated by the Horserace Totalisator Board,
163, Euston Road, London, N.W.1.

2.30.—THE BATTLE TWO-YRS-OLD SELLING PLATE

of £300; entrance £1, £1 extra if declared to run by Thursday, September 10th, and £1 in addition unless such declaration be cancelled by Saturday, September 12th; the second to receive £30 and the third £20 out of the plate; for two-yrs-old that, at starting have not won a selling race; colts, and geldings 9st 1lb., fillies 9st; the winner to be sold by auction for £100; five furlongs (24 entries, viz. 8 at £5, 7 at £3, 7 at £2 and 9 at £1).—Closed August 19th, 1964.

Jockey	st lb	Trainer	Owner
2	LITTLE GEORGE 9 3	Mrs J. A. Fisher	
	ch g Gratinade—River Kwai	D. Marks	Black and white stripes, green cap, w/fir hoop
5	COME ALIVE GREY 9 3	Mr Thomas Marshall	
	gr ro c Valmarin—Grey Marie	R. Read	Grey, blue striped sleeves, hooped cap
6	COSTA CLYDE 9 3	Mr G. Spann	
	gr c Felix of Clyde—Zaparig	G. Spann	Bottle green, orange cap and hooped slvs
7	J.K. 9 0	Mrs A. S. Beech	
	br/Le Dieu d'Or—Benediction	J. Walsh	Red, black quartered cap
8	LINSLADE 9 0	Mrs W. R. Gibson	
	b/Hook Money—Flora	R. Smyth	Claret, grey cross-belts and sleeves
9	RANSOM 9 0	Dr A. Jones	
	ch f Hook Money—Scarlet Sash	A. Jones	Red, green hooped sleeves, white cap
11	MONKS BREW 9 0	Mr H. D. Ree	
	ch f Delirium—Benedictar	W. Combes	Emerald green, maroon cap and hooped sleeves
15	YORKETTA 9 0	Mrs May Whittles	
	b or b/Chetan II—Smarty II	I. Benstead	Blue, green and white quartered cap

EIGHT DECLARED RUNNERS

Sales of winners and claims of beaten horses are subject to the Rules of Racing governing objections in Selling Races.

NOTICES.   Flags on Number Board.

Blue	... : Riders weighed in.	White	... : Objection over-ruled.
Red	... : Objection to winner.	Green	... : Objection sustained.
Red & White	: Objection to any other placed horse.	Black & White	: Number withdrawn.

Red with White "E" : Enquiry under Rule 170 (6i).
Apprentice allowances:—Red number on White, 7lb claimed; Black number on Orange, 5lb claimed; White number on Blue, 3lb claimed.
Any alteration in weights or colours, or a horse running in hood and/or blinkers, will be notified on the Number Board.

3rd Race | Daily Double | 1 mile | Armlet—YELLOW

3.0. — THE EASTBOURNE HANDICAP PLATE

of £500; entrance £2, £2 extra if declared to run by Thursday, September 10th, and £1 in addition unless such declaration be cancelled by Saturday, September 12th; the second to receive £100 and the third £50 out of the plate; for three-yr-old only which have not won a race up to the time of closing; lowest handicap weight not less than 7st; weights published Thursday, September 3rd, but a winner after Monday, August 31st, to carry 7lb, (if two races, or of one value £500 17lb extra; one mile (45 entries, one mile (45 entries, viz. 10 at £5, 9 at £4 and 25 at £2).—Closed August 19th, 1964.

Jockey	st	lb	Owner	Trainer
3	SONG OF PRAISE	8	5	Mr F. A. Laker	R. Smyth
	ch c Grantull—Sonnet			White, red cross-belts, red cap, black hoop	
7	INCOMPARABLE	8	3	Mr F. E. Hardy	R. Read
	gr g Imparcable—Contrast			Violet, cerise cross-belts, quartered cap	
8	MONTEREY	7	12	Mr F. Dell	D. Marks
	ch c Mustassid—Sphere			White, Royal blue stripe and cuffs, quartered cap	
10	OLDBURY LAD	7	10	Mr C. Knott	C. Benstead
	b or br c Right Boy—Oldbury Market			Pink, gold spots, blue collar and cuffs, red and yellow quartered cap	
11	QARAZAN	7	10	Sir John Meacock	J. Meacock
	b c Le Dieu d'Or—Roulymai			Maroon, gold sleeves, quartered cap	
12	JOLLY JINKS	7	10	Mr C. Crook	T. Corbett
	b f Tudor Jinks—Far Oasis			Light blue, pink sleeves and striped cap	
13	FISHY STORY	7	7	Mrs R. C. Brown	T. Gates
	b f King's Bench—Rock Med			Scarlet, white cross-belts and armlets, quartered cap	
16	MISCALCULATION	7	7	Major Philip Magor	T. Masson
	ch f Tamble—Thoroughput			Purple, gold star, slvs and hooped cap	
17	RE SURE	7	0	Mr F. L. Hill	M. Feakes
	ch f Arctic Siam—Re Fortune			Petunia, gold sleeves, green cap	
19	DRACULA'S DAUGHTER	7	0	Mr T. D. Grimes	D. Hanley
	ch f Hook Money—Fidelia			Grey, orange sleeves and spots on cap	

TEN DECLARED RUNNERS

The Management reserve the right to refuse admission to, or to eject, any person without assigning a reason.

The names of trainers and the pedigrees and descriptions of horses have been added for the convenience of the public, but are not guaranteed to be correct.

4th Race | Treble Event | 1 mile and a half | Armlet—GREEN

3.30. — THE DITCHLING STAKES

with £400 added in a sweepstakes of £2, £1 extra if declared to run by Thursday, September 10th, and £1 in addition unless such declaration be cancelled by Saturday, September 12th, the second to receive 20% and the third 10% of the whole stakes, for three-yr-old and upwards which have not won a race other than a weight-for-age race of less value than £350; three-yr-old, 8st 3lb, four and upwards, 9st; mares allowed 3lb; a winner of two or more races to carry 9lb extra; horses which have never won a race allowed 7lb; one mile and a half (35 entries, viz. 5 at £4, 3 at £3 and 27 at £2).—Closed August 19th, 1964.

Jockey	Trainer		Agent	lb	Owner
3	BEACHCOMBER	D. Hanley	3	8	3	Lady Aitken
	gr or ch c Final Score—Fortiea				Violet and white (quartered), sleeves reversed
5	DON'T TELL	R. Greenhill	3	8	0	The Queen
	ch f Doutelle—Lady Godiva				Purple, gold braid, scarlet sleeves, black velvet cap with gold fringe
6	DIXIELAND	P. Ashworth	3	8	0	Mr Edward B. Benjamin
	b f Nentallah—Ragtime Band				Gold, black sleeves and diagonal stripes, black cap, gold diamond
7	DOUTEUSE	J. Gosden	3	8	0	Sir Harold Wernher
	br f Doutelle—Dickmus				Green and yellow (halved), sleeves and cap reversed
8	ARSIPE	J. Stevens	3	7	10	Mr T. W. Smith
	g g Masino—At Midan				Cerise, two black hoops, striped cap

FIVE DECLARED RUNNERS

The results and starting prices at this and other Meetings are displayed on a board in each Enclosure but the Management accept no responsibility for their accuracy.

PRIZE MONEY FOR 1964

GIVEN by the Horserace Betting Levy Board **£6,101**

RETURN TRAINS

To Victoria and London Bridge ... ... 4.51 (Special), 4.56 and 5.57
(Change at East Croydon for London Bridge)
To Brighton ... ... 4.48, 5.5, 5.18, 5.36 and 5.48

BRIGHTON RACES

Wednesday & Thursday, September 16th & 17th

117

4.0. — THE MOUNTFIELD COURT NURSERY HANDICAP PLATE

of £504; entrance £2, £2 extra is declared to run by Thursday, September 10th, and £1 in addition unless such declaration be cancelled by Saturday, September 12th; the second to receive £100 and the third £50 out of the plate; for two-yr-old only; lowest handicap weight not less than 7lb; weights published Thursday, September 3rd. Just a winner after Monday, August 31st, to carry 7lb, of two races, or of one value £400 10lb extra; one mile (78 entries, viz. 13 at £5, 19 at £4 and 35 at £2).—Closed August 19th, 1964.

Jockey	#	st	lb	Owner	Trainer
1	WARD DRILL — ch c Pali Mall—Ward Sister	8	10	Mr David Robinson, Green, red sleeves, light blue cap	B. Hobbs
4	ROSA GAY — b f Stephanotis—Gay Rosalinda	8	8	Mr D. Morris, Orange, black epaulets and cap	H. Wallington
6	PROMISE — b f Democratic—White Diamond	8	8	Maj.-Gen. J. A. d'Avigdor-Goldsmid, Black and red (halved diagonally), old gold sash and cap	S. Ingham
7	McCORMACK — b g Immortality—Mrs Killeen	8	8	Duke of Norfolk, Sky blue, sky blue and scarlet qrtd cap	Sir G. Smyth
8	NIMBLE MISS — b f Nimbus—Accretion	8	2	Mr William Hill, Maroon, pale blue and maroon hooped sleeves, quartered cap	Sir G. Richards
9	WEE SPOT — b f Nectar—Kilspara	8	1	Mr David Robinson, Green, red sleeves, light blue cap	B. Hobbs
12	ROCKHAMPTON — ch g Rockefella—Bloomsbury Rose	7	10	Mr C. A. F. Sayer, Scarlet, white sash, black sleeves, red and black quartered cap	J. Bartholomew
14	ENCHANTED — br f Emus—Weird Legend	7	9	Mr T. Robinson, Orange, black striped sleeves, check cap	T. Masson
15	MARLHURST — b c Yalwara—Marly Roll	7	9	Mr J. de las Casas, Gold, brown sash, green and gold qrtd cap	E. Bamstead
16	TWICE — b f Abide—Twee Fold	7		Lady Zia Wernher, Green and yellow (halved), sleeves reversed, yellow cap	J. Gosden
17	CANADIAN CURRENCY — ch f Cash and Courage—Prairie Star	7		Mrs T. Gates, Dark grey, light grey sleeves, pink sash and cap	T. Gates
19	FLIGHT — b f Court Harwell—Track Event	7	4	Mr J. O'G. Cameron, Cameron tartan, light blue sleeves and cap with tartan hoop	K. Lundell
21	ROYAL CREST — b or br f Pali Mall—Over the Ridge	7	0	Mr V. G. Sheran, Cerise and white diagonal stripes, white cap	F. Armstrong

THIRTEEN DECLARED RUNNERS

4.30.—THE ERIDGE PARK TWO-YRS-OLD PLATE

of £509; entrance £2, £2 extra if declared to run by Thursday, September 10th, and £1 in addition unless such declaration be cancelled by Saturday, September 12th; the second to receive £100 and the third £50 out of the plate; for two-yr-old only; being maidens at the time of starting; colts and geldings 9st 0lb, fillies 8st 11lb; five furlongs (to enter, viz. 8 at £5, 13 at £4 and 48 at £2).—Closed August 19th, 1964.

Jockey	#	st	lb	Owner	Trainer
2	KUFRA — b c Royal Palm—Gay Princess	9	3	Mr H. W. Blyth, White, scarlet braid, collar and cap	F. Maxwell
5	CHAPLIN — ch g Denver—Minstrel Queen	9	3	Capt. T. E. Langton, Royal blue, silver diamond hoop, pale blue cap	D. Whelan
9	BOODLE — ch c Hook Money—Lansdamber	9		Mr R. F. Watson, Purple and green stripes and cap	Sir G. Richards
11	MINYTO — b f King's Bench—Miss Radimi	9	0	Mrs L. R. Bawtrin, Purple and primrose stripes, check cap	R. Smyth
13	MISS RHONDDA — ch f Pakistan—Tultra	9	0	Mrs L. Cohen, Sate blue and white (quartered), white sleeves	T. Masson
15	NIGHT SIGNAL — ch f Exmus—Radie Flare	9	0	Mr H. J. Joel, Black, scarlet cap	J. Sirett
18	CARIAD — b f Abbs—Lime Pay	9	0	Mr S. H. Supple, Green, red sleeves, green and white striped cap	J. Bartholomew
20	FINAL BRIDGE — b f Welsh Abbot—Pontoon	9	0	Mrs R. A. Thrale, Pale blue, wine stripe, cuffs and peak of cap	R. Thrale

EIGHT DECLARED RUNNERS

Every discerning Racegoer takes

COXFORM RACE RATINGS

Every race expertly assessed for you and will include a special staking plan for the best betting races of the day

Obtainable from : * Racecourse Bookstalls
* Our man on the Course
* 55 Curzon St., W.1. (callers only)

and by postal subscription to

COXFORM LTD., 65 New St., Birmingham 2

Miss Rhondda the winner of the Eridge Park Two-Years-Old Plate, the very last race on 14th September 1964. Seen here in the winner's enclosure, where jockey Bobby Elliott has unsaddled her and is walking away to the weighing room. Miss Rhondda was owned by L Cohen and trained at Barn Stables by Tom Masson.

above: Astley House (c.1900)   (fco:Barbican House Museum)
centre: Horses exercising in the yard of Astley House 1890s
below: 'Astley House' in its current incarnation – photo taken in 2012

7

TRAINING FACILITIES

O nce Lewes could boast some fifteen training establishments
distributed around the town – with at least six of those
contained with a square half mile at the western end of the town
– and as many as four hundred horses resident at any one time.
These seem to have 'stayed the course' through changes of
trainers and owners until recent urban development razed their
legacy to the ground.

Astley House, Spital Road, was at varying times, the base of
several notable trainers: Brown, Drewitt, Prince, Escott and
Poole. The site seems originally to have been the property of
racehorse trainer, Thomas Brown, when it consisted of 'training
stables, six cottages and a paddock' and employed a considerable
staff. It appears he also acted as Clerk of the Course at Lewes
during the 1840s. The property was auctioned in two lots by
Brown's executors in 1843 and ultimately purchased by J S
Douglas (of Chilston Castle, Kent) who 'much improved' the
stables and put in Dick Drewitt to manage them. By 1899 Escott
had moved to the premises and applied for planning permission
to add internal stabling for thirteen horses in the yard at what was
now referred to as Astley House and considered by some to be
the best yard in Lewes. Entering the big gates at the western end,
the indoor stabling (cage boxes/American barn style) was on the
left, and the facility could house over twenty horses.

Placed as it was between Spital and de Montfort Roads, it created a horse-shoe shaped facility which was clad with attractive diamond-shaped bricks, and had a grassed area in the middle containing a sand pit where the horses could enjoy a lovely roll. During Poole's time access to the elegant house could be gained from the cage boxes straight into the billiard room which had been added by Escott. Astley House has been the home yard of noteworthy racehorses such as Lord Clifden, Winslow, Poethlyn, Lady Mostyn and Shaun Spadah. In 1895 alone no less than eleven race winners were produced here: Prince Frederick, Blue Tint, Belle Winnie, Calaisand, Corinia II, Herbarian, Polly Morgan, Prince of Poets, Sea Salt Sweet Song and Wilton, with ten more in preparation. The yard also served as a 'remount' depot where military horses were billeted before going to war.

Trainer George Poole retired just after the war and the Council turned the house into flats, but by the mid 1950s it had all gone under the bulldozer to be replaced by Mansfield's garage. Currently the hideous industrial style construction is home to the police vehicle maintenance depot.

Before moving to Astley House, Harry Escott resided at Hillside in the Offham Road, but his 'Escotts' racing yard seems to have been at North House in North Street. Escotts was the home base of such notable horses as Skedaddle,

Hillside – 2012

Horizon, Father O'Flynn (1892 Grand National winner), St Anthony and Knight of Rhodes.

The stables adjacent to the Black Horse pub, Western Road, had a long history. Owned by John Wails, by 1836 they were a well established and notable hunting and livery stables; in 1841 a dealer in Channel Island cattle, a Mr Cooter had the black stallion Oroonoko standing there on behalf of J V Shelley; 1859 saw a very proud George Cox officially announce his purchase of the Inn and the facility and his plans to vastly improve the stabling. William Downes occupied the Black Horse stables in 1895 – he later constructed the Leicester Road stables – and in the first half of the 20th century it was occupied by the remarkable Lewes Butchers family of trainers starting with George, then his son Leslie, then Don. The stables were demolished in the 1960s and replaced with ugly office accommodation for income tax administrators. Now it houses welfare services.

Black Horse Inn yard with current buildings (photo 2012).

Black Horse Inn yard 1896

An 'old building' converted in 1901 to stabling by J G Gordon Woodhouse, the Elms has been through several incarnations. The original 1901 conversion created four loose boxes on the ground

floor with a central doorway (see opening to the right of the bay window today) and upstairs were three rooms with a loft to the right (the right end dormer window was once the loft access door). In the war the

View of Elms House from the entrance gate – taken 2012

building was used as a fire service base. Then known as Southover Stables the property was purchased in 1948 by John 'Towser' Gosden and at some point additional stables were added extending towards the road from the right hand end of the house. This facility was home for some time to the successful horse, Aggressor.

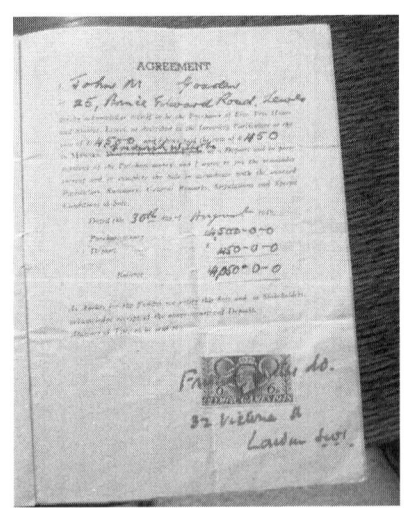

fco Mrs A Thomas

After Gosden left, the building was converted into a dwelling with the left hand original loose boxes and store room becoming a lovely sitting room (bay window). The other stables are also converted to living accommodation, dining room and kitchen, but in a way that keeps faith with the original stables and tack room.

The racing stables in Leicester Road were created in 1903 by William Downes. Around an open courtyard he built a large brick and tile rectangle which provided stabling for 25 horses plus a saddle room, coach house and store. The site also provided some grazing for the horses with its own paddocks. The facility became the base of Tom Gates who lived in the nearby house South Ellis, and later was occupied by Roger Hoad.

Leicester Road yard 1960s
fro Roger Hoad

The Leicester Road yard wall left intact (photo 2012)

As a culmination of standing empty for a few years, the yard suffered the indiscriminate ravages of the 1987 hurricane when stable roofs were ripped off and the whole facility became terminally damaged. Ultimately the yard was razed to the ground except for the curtain 15ft wall, to be replaced by new housing known as Wallands Park Rise. The original yard access from Leicester Road still serves to provide access to the residences. The Planning record of 2004 shows that the "*application site, a former racing stables, is located on land between Prince Edwards Road,*

Leicester Road and Abergavenny Road. The site covers an area of approximately 0.3 ha. The eastern part of the site, to the rear of Abergavenny Road, is presently undeveloped and vacant, having been last used as grazing land in connection with the stables, which are located on the western part of the site behind the properties in Leicester Road. The stables are contained within a retaining wall that rises up to 5 metres on the southern boundary adjacent to Shelley Close."

Nunnery Stables on the corner of de Montfort Road and Irelands Lane, has been occupied by many trainers including Alfred Sydney, Jock Langland, Tom Fitton, Matt Feakes, Towser Gosden, Renee Emery, Gordon Smyth, the lady trainer Auriol Sinclair and finally Bobby Beasley. The Nunnery housed 23 horses in its indoor stabling which is now a block of flats with small yards which were once the loose boxes – manger rings can still be seen on the walls.

Manger rings still in the walls of the courtyards which were once loose boxes

Aggressor at The Nunnery c.1959
fco Don Byrne

Left: The Nunnery flats viewed
from de Montfort Road 2012

Barn Stables in the 1930s; note Tom Masson on the right

from the collection of Bob Butchers

Barn Stables in de Montfort Road also has a long history. In 1899 it was still Spital Barn but in 1930 George Poole (then at adjacent Astley House) applied for planning for loose boxes.

Later the converted barns were to become Tom Masson's yard where he kept some of the royal horses. After Tom's death it was taken over by his son, Michael, who produced the 1970 Cheltenham Triumph Hurdle winner, Varma; and Midsummer Star who broke the track record at Folkestone.

Barn Stables conversion – interior of yard/courtyard – 2012

Barn Stables is now flats which mercifully have been rather tastefully converted. The adjoining open area to the east, now used as a car park, was formerly a slaughterhouse and then a dairy.

Winterbourne was initially a stock farm which became a stud farm in the capable hands of H Heasman in the late 1800s and then training stables for the Fitton brothers and Thomas F Smith. Tom Masson also rented some boxes there for six or so of his overspill and so did Towser Gosden and Bob Moore. Auriol Sinclair would also rent boxes when she had overspill or horses that needed to rest because of injury – the Winterbourne stream was ideal for paddling lame horses for water-therapy.

Winterbourne in 1973
with the 1930s housing estate creeping up.

The land is now covered with a housing estate; some buildings still exist which have been converted to residences known as Winterbourne Mews; most of the curtain wall remains and the house is still there in private ownership. The Winterbourne Stream is included in the Lewes Railwaylands Wildlife Park so at least its immediate vicinity seems secure for the moment.

Nevill Road, a two-storey stable block nearly opposite Victoria Hospital, was occupied in 1915 by William Downes, then Don Butchers, then Tim O'Sullivan and in 1948 by Harry Hannon and later by Tom Gates for his overspill. Again, long since gone under the construction industry's relentless bulldozer and replaced by housing but, alongside the steps, the slope up to Nevill Road once used by the horses is still there.

New Level Stables, North Street (near the Fire Station) was the yard of Fred Marshall whose foremost concern was his riding school, but he also had the racehorse Plum Jam, who was so successful at Plumpton that a race there is named after her. Bob Moore also trained from New Level.

New Level shared the general fate of Lewes's stable yards and was demolished. The site is now an industrial park which itself is currently destined for demolition and reconstruction

the New Level yard (fco Roger Hoad)

walking back from the gallops down North Street to New Level Stables (fco Roger Hoad)

The re-sited Town Mill aka Shelley's Mill, adjacent to the Prison
later to become Heath House Stables and then
Windmill Lodge Racing Stables

In 1895 Jonathan Riste at the stables of Pelham House, made a planning application to build stabling at 'Town Mill' in the Spital[10] Road. Town Mill had been moved from its original site in Pipe Passage in the early 1800s to the Spital site, where it was worked until 1858 for the Smart family (and known as Smart's Mill) and after that for the Shelley family and known as Shelley's Mill. Riste was granted permission to construct 18 loose boxes in an L-shape with a service passageway in front. The miller's cottage was either replaced or enlarged gradually becoming referred to as Heath House at the turn of the 19/20th century. The whole facility was leased by Harry Escott of Astley House in 1909. The year 1912

---

[10] Spital is the mediaeval word for hospital (sometimes spelt Spittle), which would fit at Lewes because the mediaeval infectious diseases hospital St Nicholas's, was located at the western end of town – as is the Victoria Hospital today.

saw the removal of the sweeps and smock from the now disused windmill and the Marquis of Abergavenny purchased the site in 1914, subsequently leasing it to George Poole and finally selling it to him in 1922 – the year Shaun Spadah won the Grand National. In 1930 Eric Stedall applied for planning to create portable loose boxes at Heath House, which are now residences. Auctioned in 1949 it came into the ownership of R Maxwell when the house had seven bedrooms, the current dining room was stabling and the windmill was serving as a barn. Heath House survived through several more changes of ownership, alterations and functions, and was acquired by John 'Towser' Gosden in 1960. Towser undertook further constructional improvements and added new stables creating accommodation for 25 horses. Harry Hannon also trained from the Heath House complex. Auriol Sinclair used a large number of boxes adjacent to the windmill and actually used the windmill itself as one big box for convalescing injured or unwell horses. Gordon Smyth acquired it in 1965 and later applied to build five more loose boxes; in 1970 he had an indoor riding arena constructed and further hay storage buildings. He used the dysfunctional windmill as a tack room. At one point the complex could house up to sixty horses.

Later Bob Beeson trained from this facility with 40 horses, and Bob Streeter, one of his team, recalls that then the windmill was utilised as a feed room.

Around 1983 the yard became divided, and the lower yard at the house was converted to residences, and the windmill block became a separate training yard – the eponymous centre of Windmill Lodge Stables.

Heath House yard before
separation of windmill

Heath House stables now housing 2013

In 1986 trainer Roger Hoad gained planning permission to convert the windmill into the rather handsome residence it is today surrounded by the loose boxes of the training facility of the Hoad family.

Roger's son Mark now holds the licence and races in France as well as the UK with horses such as Mafeking and Majestueux.

Windmill Lodge Racing Stables 2013

The stables in Paddock Lane have seen service as the carriage and coach horse housing for the Shelley family and for the Royal Mail stagecoach service between Lewes and Haywards Heath. George Poole used its four boxes and two coach houses as a secondary yard. The successful hurdler called Shafe and a good flat runner called The Bog were kept here. Now dedicated to art, one of the loose boxes is used as a studio and still called The Stable.

Over the years several trainers also utilised the stabling at the Pelham Arms – a public house owned by The Duke of Newcastle in the 1730s, which adopted Pelham Arms as its name in 1790. In addition there was stabling at The Swan Inn and the Coach House (now housing) in Southover High Street.

This is by no means an exhaustive summary of all the training establishments that have ever been in Lewes. Though the yards with 20 to 60 horses are well remembered and sometimes documented, there were also many smaller places that had a just five or so. After the war many ex-cavalry officers started training with a handful of horses, and there was the local nobility who chose to have a private trainer at their own premises. The record is scant enough on the big and famous yards, so next to invisible for the smaller private places.

All the foregoing had the benefit of Lewes's exceptional selection of fine gallops – reputedly the oldest dedicated gallops in Europe which are, and were, an asset without measure for those trainers and horses based at Lewes.

The basic necessity of good gallops – all within very easy reach of every yard – was well catered for and after closure the actual course became a gallop in as well.

The Rails gallop was part of the original racecourse and once had iron railings which were removed to melt down for ammunition in the war. This gallop was also improved by gangs of prisoners from the adjacent Lewes Gaol, who dug up the top soil down to the chalk, laid peat moss and then replaced the top soil and turf; later Towser Gosden put his staff and son John to making further such improvements to create a wonderful summer gallop. Even now the traces of these efforts can still be seen in the greener appearance of that side of the gallop and improved going for the horses.

Later the stretch of the Well gallop from the Well Bottom to Hurdle Hill benefited from the establishment of an all-weather surface put in by T.P. McGovern when he was at Grandstand Stables.

The Rails gallop 2013

the Well Gallop in 1891

The Well Gallop, I.S & D News, 1891

Five furlong gallop from Mill to Mill (Illustrated Sporting & Dramatic News 1891)

The Five Furlong Gallop from Mill to Mill seems to have been a stretch possibly starting at Town Mill (now Windmill Lodge next to Heath House) passing Spittle Mill (burnt down by the time of this drawing) and on to Offham Mill.

The area known as 'the foot of the hill' which is between the back of Heath House and what is now the housing development called The Gallops, was used as the assembly point for the strings of horses before going up to the gallops for their daily workout. Here the exercise jockeys would receive instructions from their trainers (who had previously been instructed by the 'chief' trainer who had charge of all the gallops), as to which gallops were to be used on that particular day and how the horses were to be ridden.

Bob Butchers recalls 'our gallops were known as Front Hill, Hurdle Hill, Balmer, Middle Hill, Inside the Racecourse, the Rails, the Well and Summer Gallop' and has recorded the regret that when he made a 'memory lane' visit to Lewes within the last few years he was dismayed by the changes, by places once familiar having altered beyond recognition.

2012 view down to the back of Barn Stables and Nevill Road
from mid way up the 'foot of the hill' assembly point

In particular he says: "I went to 'the foot of the hill' which is how we knew the first area of grass after entering the South Downs from the main road. The area was used to break-in [teach] yearlings, for grazing and for the assembly of training strings. Now the grass has been neatly mown, several trees planted and there are notice boards saying 'No horses allowed on this area' ... such a notice shortly after the war would have given rise to nearly 400 equine trespassers!"

Times do indeed change, and whether or not for the better is a matter for personal contemplation, but it does seem that the wholesale exchange of living horseflesh for inert metal and petroleum has impaired the human spirit as much as it has damaged the planet.

Training Yards location guide

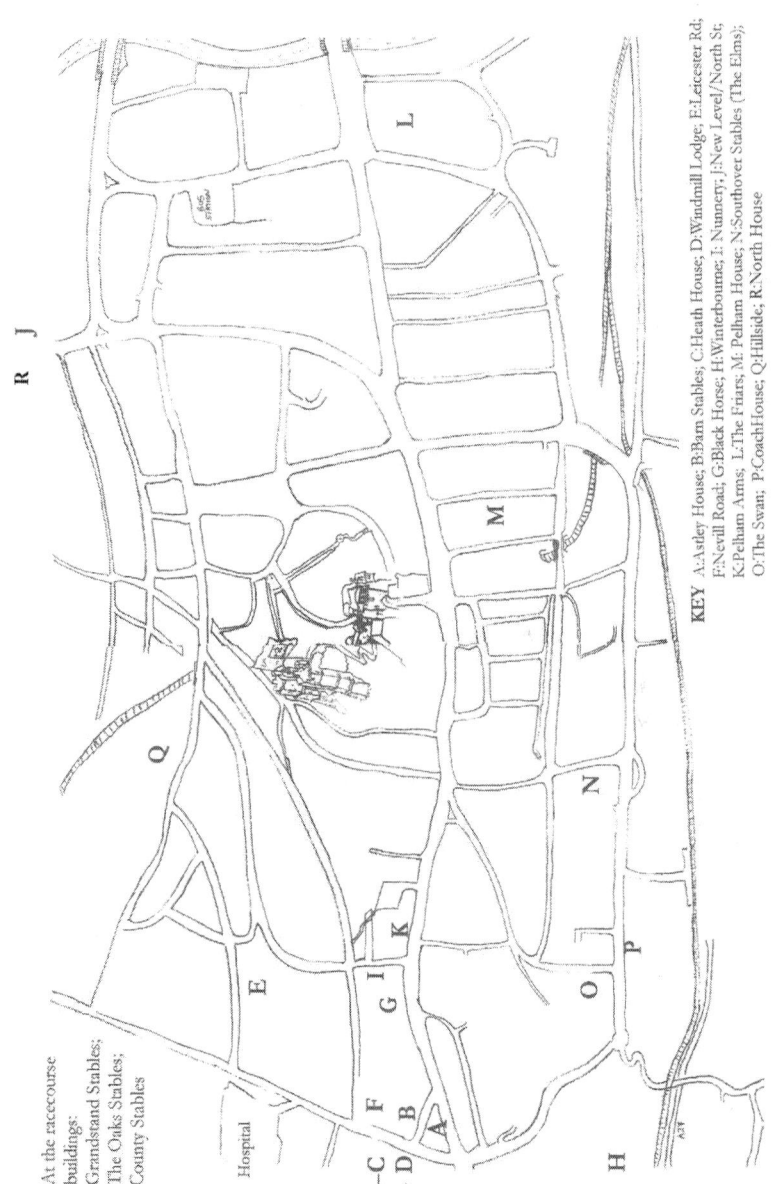

KEY A:Astley House; B:Barn Stables; C:Heath House; D:Windmill Lodge; E:Leicester Rd; F:Nevill Road; G:Black Horse; H:Winterbourne; I: Nunnery; J:New Level/North St; K:Pelham Arms; L:The Friars; M: Pelham House; N:Southover Stables (The Elms); O:The Swan; P:CoachHouse; Q:Hillside; R:North House

At the racecourse buildings:
Grandstand Stables;
The Oaks Stables;
County Stables

8

PAST THE POST

Despite it all and by dint of undaunted individuals, Lewes managed to retain its connection to the racing industry. In this it is more fortunate than the course at Gatwick which closed in June 1940 and suffered the final ignominy of being covered with airport terminals and runway tarmac, with only a restaurant name 'The Course' to vaguely recall its sporting past.

Initially after the formal closure, the Abergavenny family leased the land to local farmers and the course to Towser Gosden for gallops. In 1966 Frank Muggeridge had taken the lease of a part of the racecourse buildings, moving his establishment up there and converting the Tote building into stabling (now County Stables) and the timber weighing room into his residence. This was more of an undertaking than at first it may sound as there was no electricity and no hot water, no sewage system. Pat Mitchell said it was like camping and the novelty soon wore off! But Muggeridge went on to produce some successful horses from the defunct course, including the last horse from Lewes to run in the King George VI Chase at Kempton Park: Shawnigan achieved third place at 100-1 ridden by Paul Kelleway.

Always able to see the amusing side, Muggeridge declared "Thank God he didn't win. There's not enough champagne at Kempton for the party we would have enjoyed".

In 1971 to finance death duties, the Abergavenny family sold the 700 acres, course and buildings. The whole lot was purchased by a property developer, Arthur Bourne, who had plans for the buildings and an enormous housing estate in mind for Houndean Bottom, which did not come to pass and all was sold to an assurance company. Without going into the minutiae of varying exchanges of freehold, etc., suffice to say that the buildings were left empty and decaying until ultimately acquired by Nick Cheyney after a time-and-chance encounter. He recalls: *"In the 1980s a group of us would regularly meet up to run over the South Downs. One misty Sunday on the Lewes stretch we were surprised by a ruinous collection of dilapidated buildings eerily emerging as we approached. The following Sunday we met again and a newspaper advertisement was brought to my attention – that site was up for sale. It seemed like fate so I made an offer and ended up buying the whole site. Later I converted the principal building into a home for my family and sold off the rest."*

Subsequently, John Ffitch-Heyes purchased much of it, and when the assurance company sold their holdings he acquired parts of that and so did Dick West. The latter ultimately sold his to the district council and Ffitch-Heyes sold the course with buildings in 2002. Some buildings enjoyed a new life as stabling and others as dwellings for those connected with the racing stables. It is a nice touch that several are named after horses significant to the course, such as Rhylstone, Manhattan Cottage and Charlottown Cottage. The superstructure of the second grandstand is now three residences, and a building that is thought to have been the Judge's Box is in the process of conversion into a single house. The racecourse and remaining buildings now provide the backdrop to a thriving and very busy training centre with four racing establishments currently based there.

Grandstand Stables. John Ffitch-Heyes used this facility first, then it was bought by Tom P McGovern. He trained Eastwell Hall, a strong contender for the 1999 and 2000 Cesarewitch. One apprentice recalls Tom as a great character and "one of the nicest people I ever worked for". McGovern, who in early 2002 was the only active trainer at the racecourse, is on record as saying that "It is a lovely bit of turf. You couldn't ask for better facilities." He was still there in 2003 but suffering from arthritis so ultimately retired.

The Oaks Racing Stables is the base of trainer Gerry Enright, who undertook his apprenticeship with Gordon Smyth between 1966 and 1971. Enright describes Smyth as a very well-spoken disciplinarian who did not take kindly to misdemeanours of stable lads. Having accidentally broken a small piece of glass in a high level fanlight window Gerry was instantly docked a month's wages. Later he became a flat race jockey with Arthur Stephenson for a year and then a National Hunt jockey with Josh Gifford until 1986 for whom he rode Nougat, the winner of the Imperial Cup in 1975 among others. Upon taking up training himself, he acquired the Oaks Stables at Lewes racecourse. Among the winners he has trained on Front of Hill and All Through Gallops have been Indian Baba, Golden Fox and High Point. During my visit Gerry looked out at the splendid view from his kitchen window and through a plume of pipe smoke, remarked in his warm Irish accent, "this is an amazing place; it's a privilege to be here". Mrs Enright pointed out that she thought it quite unique that from the top of the downs slightly to the north no less than three racecourses could be seen: Lewes at your feet; Plumpton to the north; Brighton to the west.

In 2002 Suzy Smith established herself at Frank Muggeridge's original facility, County Stables, and for her gallops she uses the actual racecourse currently owned by David Marsh. Originally the Tote Building, County Stables houses 20 horses. Suzy is well known for her production of the one-eyed mare, Material World, who after an operation to remove an infected eye went on to win several races in fine style, 'cruising home in isolation' as one reporter put it. Material World has since started another career as a brood mare and can even boast her own web site! Suzy has lately expanded her game plan to take advantage of the greater prize money across the Channel, regularly boxing the horses on the ferry and participating in France. She said, "We like to do it differently, I believe racing should be fun and we try to keep it that way for our owners, the horses and ourselves." One of the horses recently in her charge was Join The Dots, who was, as they say, a horse of a different colour in that he had white patches in his brown coat, which is unusual in Thoroughbreds. Currently Suzy is enjoying success with Natural Spring and Emma's Legend.

Since 2005 Grandstand Stables, together with the ten furlong Rails gallop, has been the base of Jim and Tom Best. Both had started in racing very young and rode at the yards of Richard Rowe and Josh Gifford. Upon moving into training, they acquired their 30-horse Lewes facility, and in their first full season catapulted up the trainers' league into the top five in the UK. In 2009 they took the step of creating a one-mile all-weather gallop alongside the existing and historic Rails – the same gallop that has resounded to the hoof beats of Aggressor and Charlottown, being previously used by John Towser Gosden, and later by trainer Gordon Smyth. Jim and Tom take the view that: "This is a good place for us. We have had nearly 200 winners from here and are fortunate not only because we have the two superb gallops, and training jumps, but for fitness work we have access to open downland which also makes a nice change for the horses. We enjoy it too."

These trainers – together with Mark Hoad at Windmill Lodge – are all routinely racing their horses and doing a grand job of keeping the famous racing name of Lewes on the racing map.

Of course, no one can predict the future of anything. As this chapter is being prepared the fates of two other racecourses have been decided – Hereford and Folkestone are to close. Hereford's prospects are unclear, but Folkestone has been sold to developers to create a gargantuan housing estate.

Though most of the original Lewes stable yards have been wiped away, at least the course, the gallops and professional trainers are still maintaining the town's legacy in the traditional aspects of British life and sport. Hence what seemed to be the final and tragic demise of a much loved racecourse in 1964 has transpired to keep it still breathing fifty years later, thanks not to any atypical foresight of planners or civic pride, but to the initiative of individuals. As the 2014 joint anniversaries of the Battle of Lewes and of the closure of the racecourse reflect, history is not only the past but part of the present ... and future, which itself will ultimately become history.

Aerial views courtesy of Peter Fellows
above: the racecourse buildings;
below looking west over the course and parts of the gallops

APPENDICES

Appendix I | ROYAL PLATES at LEWES, SUSSEX

*1720 The King's Plate, won by FOX
*1722 The King's Plate, won by LAMPREY
*1723 The King's Plate, won by RED ROSE
*1724 The King's Plate, won by TICKLE ME QUICKLY
1727 His Majesty's Plate of 100gs, for six yrs. old horses, carrying 12st - SAMPSON (w/o)
1728 A Plate of 100gs, for six yrs. old horses, carrying 12st, 4-mile heats – GOLIATH
1729 His Majesty's Plate of 100gs, for six yrs. old horses, carrying 12st, 4-mile heats –
THUNDERBOLT (w/o)
1730 His Majesty's Plate of 100gs, for 6 yr old horses, carrying 12st, 4-mile heats – TARRAN
1731 His Majesty's Plate of 100gs, for six yrs. old horses, carrying 12st - GREYLEGS
1732 His Majesty's Plate of 100gs, for 6 yr old horses, carrying 12st, 4-mile heats – DIAMOND
1733 His Majesty's Plate of 100gs, for six yrs. old horses, 12st, 4-mile heats - STARLING
1734 His Majesty's Plate of 100gs, for six yrs. old horses, carrying 12st, 4-mile heats - SLY
1735 His Majesty's Plate of 100gs, for 6yr old horses, 12st, 4-mile heats –
JENNY-COME-TIE-ME
1736 His Majesty's Plate of 100gs, for 6 yr olds, carrying 12st, 4-mile heats – MERRY ANDREW
1737 His Majesty's Plate of 100gs, for six yrs. old horses, 12st, 4-mile heats - GRASSHOPPER
1738 His Majesty's Plate – BLACK CHANCE
1739 His Majesty's Plate of 100gs, 12st, 4-mile heats - BLAZE
1740 His Majesty's Plate of 100gs, for six yrs. old, 12st, 4-mile heats - ELEPHANT
1741 His Majesty's Plate, 12st, 4-mile heats – POOR ROBIN
1742 His Majesty's Plate of 100gs, for six yrs. old horses, 12st, 4-mile heats - SOURFACE
1743 His Majesty's Plate of 100gs, for six yrs. old, 12st, 4-mile heats - ACHILLES
1744 His Majesty's Plate of 100gs, for six yrs. old, 12st, 4-mile heats - STARLING
1745 His Majesty's Plate of 100gs, 4-mile heats - REGULUS
1746 His Majesty's Plate of 100gs, for six yrs. old, 12st, 4-mile heats – SLOE (w/o)
1747 His Majesty's Plate of 100gs, six yrs horses, 4-mile heats – CUMBERLAND (w/o)
1748 His Majesty's Plate of 100gs – STADHOLDER
1749 His Majesty's Plate of 100gs, 4-mile heats - OTHELLO
1750 His Majesty's Plate of 100gs, for six yrs. old, 12st, 4-mile heats - STUMP
1751 His Majesty's 100gs, for six yrs. old, carrying 12st - SAMPSON
1752 The King's Plate of 100gs, for six yrs. old, 12st – TRAVELLER
1753 The King's Plate of 100gs, for six yrs. old, 12st – SPORTSMAN (w/o)
1754 The King's 100gs, for six yrs. old, 12st – CATO
1755 The King's 100gs, for six yrs. old, 12st - JASON (w/o)
1756 The King's 100gs, for six yrs. old, 12st – ADOLPHUS (w/o)
1757 The King's 100gs, for six yrs. old, 12st - CARELESS
1758 The King's 100gs, for six yrs. old, 12st – JACK-OF-NEWBURY
1759 The King's 100gs, for six yrs. old, 12st, 4-mile heats - DORMOUSE
1760 The King's 100gs, for six yrs. old, 12st, 4-mile heats – BOSPHORUS (w/o)
1761 The King's 100gs, for six yrs. old, 12st, 4-mile heats - APOLLO
1762 The King's 100gs, for six yrs. old, 12st, 4-mile heats – BOREAS (w/o)
1763 The King's 100gs, for six yrs. old, 12st, 4-mile heats - HAVANNAH
1764 The King's Plate of £100, for six yrs. old, 12st, 4-mile heats - CYCLOPS
1765 The King's 100gs, for six yrs. old, 12st, 4-mile heats – STAR

Appendix II | Horses that won more than four times at Lewes

Andy	1928	Club Welter Handicap
	1929	Members Welter Handicap
	1930	De Warrenne Handicap
	1931	Members Welter Handicap
	1931	Club Welter Handicap
	1932	Members Welter Handicap
	1932	Hamsey Welter Handicap
	1934	Club Welter Handicap
Breada	1886	Club Open Handicap
	1887	Southdown Club Open Handicap
	1887	Lewes Autumn Handicap
	1888	Lewes Spring Handicap
	1888	Ashcombe Handicap
	1889	Southdown Club Cup
Confusion	1863	Borough Members Plate
	1864	Handicap Selling Stakes
	1864	Selling Stakes
	1865	Selling Stakes
	1865	A Handicap
Lady Mostyn	1875	Astley Stakes
	1875	Priory Stakes
	1876	Lewes Spring Handicap
	1878	Hamsey Welter Handicap
	1878	Town Plate
Charity Concert	1948	Hamsey Handicap
	1948	Apprentices Plate
	1949	Hamsey Handicap
	1950	Hamsey Handicap
Fraulein	1874	Nevill Stakes
	1874	Corinthian Handicap
	1875	Lewes Spring Handicap
	1875	Lewes Grand Handicap
Operatic Society	1959	Sussex Plate
	1959	Pevensey Handicap
	1963	Southdown Plate
	1964	Southdown Plate
Red Pippin	1951	Hamsey Handicap
	1951	Ashdown Welter Handicap
	1952	Hamsey Handicap
	1954	Beacon Handicap

Appendix III | Pratt & Co

Pratt & Co were a company involved in the administration of racecourses and racing. They were established in the early 1870s by John Pratt and a Mr Bell. In 1881 the partnership was joined by Mr George Verrall of Lewes. They had a number of racecourses under their management, including Cheltenham, Fontwell Park, Gatwick, Plumpton, Alexandra Park, Folkestone and, of course, Lewes. They would supply the officials required on the days of racing and would collect the entrance fees and deal with other financial transactions on the day, making the whole process of racing so much easier for all concerned. Mr Frederick Henry Cathcart joined them in 1894 and his name can be seen on Lewes race cards as the Clerk of the Course; he also became the first Chairman of the Cheltenham Steeplechase Company, and is credited with transforming the fortunes of that racecourse. The Bloodstock Breeders' Review obituary recorded: "In the racing world of today there is no man imbued with a greater spirit of enterprise than Mr Cathcart. If he could have his way the Turf would quickly undergo developments of a striking and beneficial character."

George Verrall died in 1911 and his nephew Ernest Robinson replaced him. Robinson had strong connections with the Jockey Club going back through generations of his family to 1806.

It seems Pratt & Co were a good firm to work for as they benefitted from loyal and long-serving staff, including two who were with them for fifty years.

Appendix IV | Sussex Ox

Curiously, Professor Long writing about Sussex Cattle in *The Encyclopaedia of Modern Agriculture* quoted Lord Sheffield as having said that at the end of the 18th century an ox of the Sussex breed travelled over the four-mile racecourse at Lewes in 16 minutes. A very remarkable ox indeed but it begs the question "why?" was he asked to undertake this feat.

Lewes racecourse was not exclusive to Thoroughbred horses and has been used for several alternative purposes over the years. For example, in September 1922 The Great Arabian Endurance Test was contested from Lewes Racecourse to Arundel, organised by the Arab Horse Society. The horses each carried thirteen stone, and had to cover a route of 60 miles on each of five consecutive days – from Lewes to Arundel and back again. Half a dozen horses competed and in the first day's test with Mr H V Musgrave Clark's mare Belka, who was the 1921 winner, Mr S G Hough's stallion Shahzada, and the gelding Robin, completed in a period of seven hours, exclusive of compulsory stoppages. Shahzada was later exported to Australia where the great 250-mile Shahzada Endurance Ride was named after him.

Lewes is also on the record for motor racing. The **Lewes Speed Trials** were held on a stretch of road on Race Hill known as "The Motor Road." The first meeting on July 27, 1924, was organised by the Brighton & Hove Motor Cycle and Light Car Club, on a quarter-mile course. Fastest time of the day was set by J.A. Hall, Frazer Nash-GN, in a time of 16.6 secs. Thereafter speed trials were held on the Race Hill three or four times a year from 1925 to 1939, organised by the Brighton & Hove MC, the Kent & Sussex LCC, the Bugatti Owners' Club and the Vintage Sports Car Club. Jean Bugatti attended the races on 21 October 1933; Denis Jenkinson, motor racing journalist, attended his first motor sport event here in 1936. *The Autocar* magazine reported from the meeting in June 1937 that "The first appearance in competition of the new four-wheel independent-suspension Atalanta was at Lewes."

Appendix VI | Pilot and jockey

On 28th August 1940 a Gotha Go.145B German mail plane was forced to land by two Hurricanes who had spotted him when he lost his way on his journey from Germany to the Channel Islands. The German pilot landed his plane safely at Lewes Racecourse.

The somewhat bemused and scared pilot was taken away by the authorities and interestingly his name was Leonhard Buikle – the German rendition of the surname Buckle. One hundred years earlier in 1806 Frank Buckle had ridden Sancho on the course in a famous match race.

Appendix VII | Telscombe Village

The eminent Shelley family of Lewes held the manor of Telscombe until the late 1800s. Then in 1893 it came into the hands of Ambrose Gorham, a successful bookmaker and racehorse owner. He produced the 1904 Grand National winner, Shannon Lass from his stables there. With his winnings from that race Gorham made huge improvements to the very rural village, bringing it mains water and electricity. He also built a club to provide a social facility for the stable lads – perhaps in part to prevent them going further afield to find pubs and sell tips. That club is now the village hall. Gorham died in 1933 and left the village and its surrounding land to Brighton Corporation with the covenant that it was allowed to keep in perpetuity its rural nature and that no public house should be allowed! He was buried in St Lawrence's Church graveyard where a monument was erected in his memory.

In 1960 Fortnum & Mason's vice chairman Ernest Thornton-Smith gifted Telscombe manor house and 54 acres to the National Trust.

Appendix VIII | Some Sussex Racecourses

	first recorded	defunct by
Alfriston	1787	1798
Brighton	1783	still in operation
Gatwick	1890	1940
Hastings	1826	1867
Lewes	1714	1964
Plumpton	1884	still in operation
Fontwell	1924	still in operation
Uppark	1782	1785
Worthing	1860	1869

Several other courses can only be shown to have held one or two meetings, such as: Littlehampton where racing was on the beach in 1863; Eastbourne; Michel Grove near Arundel; Rotherfield.

~ ~ ~

ACKNOWLEDGEMENTS

Adam, Mr & Mrs David
Anne of Cleves House/Museum, Lewes
Barbican Museum, Lewes
Best, Jim
Bodle, Mrs Jacqueline (nee Windless)
Butchers, Bob
Byrne, Don
Byrne, Martin
Cairns, Bob
Carpenter, Ian
Cheyney, Nick
Cox, Timothy, The Cox Library
Crowley, Jo
Dean, Steven
East Sussex Record Office
Elliott, Bobby
Enright, Gerry
Fellows, Peter
Ffitch-Heyes, John
Goldstein, Ray
Goodwin, Mr & Mrs D
Gosden, John
Griffiths, Val
Hammond, Christopher J., MRCVS
Hoad, Roger
Hicks, Bunny

Jardine, Mr & Mrs
Marsh, Mr & Mrs David
Marshall, Warren
National Archives, Kew
National Horse Racing Museum
Piggott, Susan
Robinson, Patricia (nee Rees)
Slaughter, John
Smith, Suzy
Stenning, James
Stevens, Lawrence
Streeter, Bob
Tapp, Mrs Barbara (nee Moore)
Thomas, Mrs Ann
Walker, Ben
Walker, Jules

Bibliography

Abelson & Tyrrel, The Breedon Book of Horse Racing Records, 1993

Astley, Sir John D., Bart., *Fifty Years of My Life*, 1895

Bayles, F H, *The Race Courses Atlas of Great Britain & Ireland*,
                    Henry Faux, October 1903

Brunnarius, Martin, *The Windmills of Sussex*, Phillimore 1979

Butchers, Bob *Silks, Soaks & Certainties*, Blenheim Press Ltd, 2008

British Newspapers Archive

Clee, Nicholas, *Eclipse* Bantam Press, London, 2009

Cobbett, Martin *Wayfaring Notions*, London 1906

Collins, Digby, *The Horse-Trainers' Guide*, London, 1865

Fleetwood-Jones, Colin, *Pacemaker & The Horseman*, 1796

Gill, James, **Racecourses of Great Britain**, Barrie & Jenkins, 1975

Greaves, Ralph, *Racecourses of England*
                    Field Sports Publications 1959

Horsfield, Thomas Walker, *The History & Antiquities of Lewes &
                    Its Vicinity*, Volume 1, J Baxter, Lewes, 1824

How To Go Racing with Pleasure & Comfort in England & France, 1901

Illustrated Sporting & Dramatic News, multiple editions c 1800-1900

Lady's Magazine, Volume VI, 1835

London & Paris Observer, volume ix, 1833

Mason, Finch, *Heroes & Heroines of Grand Nationals*, Biographical
                    Press, London 1911

O'Leary, Con, *Grand National*, Rockliff, London 1945

Pitt, Chris, *A Long Time Gone*, Portway Press Ltd, 2006

Porter, John, *John Porter of Kingsclere, An Autobiography*,
                    Grant Richards Ltd, London, 1919

Radcliffe, J.B., *Ashgill: The Life & Times of John Osborne*,
                    Sand & Co, London 1900

Racing Calendar, 1777

Racing Illustrated, 1896

Richardson, C, *The English Turf: A Record of Horses & Courses*,
                    Methuen, 1901

Rickman, John, *Homes of Sport: Horse Racing*, Garnett, London, 1952

Ruffs Guide to the Turf, Sportsman Office, 1876 and 1879

Russell, Fox, *In Scarlet & Silk*, Bellairs & Co, London, 1896

Scott, Alexander, *Memories of the Turf*, Hutchinson & Co., 1849

Short Histories of Racecourses in England, Field Sports Publication

Sporting Chronicle, 1915

Sporting Clipper, 1887

Sussex Express

Taunton, Thomas Henry, MA *Portraits of Celebrated Racehorses 1702-1870*

The Turf Register and Sportsman & Breeder's Stud-Book

U3A, *Lewes Remembers Racing & Race Days*, U3A publication1994

Weatherby's, *The General Stud Book*, Volume XV

Illustrations

Many illustrations have been sourced from private/personal collections or taken especially for this book.
For the historic photographs we thank the National Horse Racing Museum in Newmarket and the Sussex Archaeological Society/Barbican House Museum which administers the Reeves, Bartlett and Bedford Collections.

Glossary

Barouche - a fashionable carriage of the 19th century; four-wheeled, low slung, it had two double seats inside, arranged so the passengers in the front seat faced those in the back seat. It had a soft collapsible half-hood folding like a bellows over the back seat and a high outside box seat in front for the driver, and was suspended on C springs. Traditionally drawn by a pair of high-quality horses, it was used principally for leisure driving in the summer.

Colt: a male horse under the age of four.

Farrier: a specialist blacksmith who shoes horses; much of the success of a horse can depend on the skill of his farrier.

Filly: a female horse under the age of four years.

Furlong: one British mile is made up of eight furlongs; a furlong therefore measures 220 yards (200 metres approx).

Gelding: a castrated male horse of any age.

Match Race: a race organised for just two horses; usually on a private basis – such as owner challenging owner.

Pitchfork: a two-pronged long handled tool used for pitching up bales of hay or straw on to a stack.

Plate – a special lightweight shoe used for duration of the race.

Quarters – the hind end of a horse, where the motor is housed!

Thoroughbred – a specific breed of horse that has been developed in England since the 1700s for galloping speed. A horse must be registered with the General Stud Book to be acknowledged as a Thoroughbred and to be allowed to race at formal British Racing Authority fixtures.

Previous publications by Cheryl R Lutring

The Allen Guides to Horse Breeds:
The American Saddlebred (2005)

Monumental Equus: Honouring the Horse (2010)

War Horse ... Biopics (2011)

In addition she writes on horses in history for magazines around the world, including *Horse & Hound*, and America's oldest and largest monthly publication *Saddle & Bridle*.

She has received international recognition for her work in enhancing public understanding of the USA's National Breed, the American Saddlebred, and the role of horses throughout the development of humankind.